110669377

"In *Sensing God*, Laurence Freeman takes us through the difficult desert days of Lent with extraordinary clarity and depth in his teaching of meditation and with his usual references to poetry, science and teachings from other faiths. (This is more than 'a beginner's guide' and could also apply to any other forty days.) For me as an artist, Laurence's teaching on Christian meditation has given me a daily practice and with it has come about a change in perception and in my studio work. It has helped me to embrace the intimacy and emptiness of silence that I find so important. On Holy Thursday he says, 'We will not be able to touch reality unless we allow it to touch us.' Much of the creative endeavor is about that touch, and the journey of meditation leads us toward it. I'm so grateful that this book has expanded that understanding and links me to the worldwide community that is also seeking it through a daily practice."

—CATHERINE GOODMAN, artist and Artistic Director of the Royal Drawing School

"All great religions have deeply rooted traditions of prayer, atonement and renewal. In *Sensing God*, Father Laurence takes us on a Christian journey of meditation that enriches and deepens the forty days of Lent. For Christians, this book will make a precious and gentle companion during the spiritual journey that Lent represents. Non-Christians will find deep and clear wisdom in his commentaries to the New Testament passages. They beam compassion and will help all of us re-centre ourselves in this age of obsessive self-centeredness."

—PHILIPP HILDEBRAND, Vice-Chairman, BlackRock

"Laurence Freeman has the ability to say profound and revelatory things in simple sentences and a convincing voice that could only come from a very clear place within. This is a rich feast that will not just feed but might just transform the reader. It will lead you through a new kind of Lent."

—RICHARD ROHR, OFM, Center for Action and Contemplation, Albuquerque, New Mexico

"The practice of meditation has enabled me to experience work as a form of service and life as a process of growth. In *Sensing God*, Father Laurence Freeman provides us with a practical—yet profound—roadmap for this inward journey."

—SEAN HAGAN, Member, WCCM Guiding Board, and General Counsel, International Monetary Fund

SENSING GOD

SENSING GOD

Learning to Meditate During Lent

Laurence Freeman, OSB

Franciscan
MEDIA
Cincinnati, Ohio

All rights reserved. No part of this book may be reproduced or transmitted in any form or by any means, electronic or mechanical, including photocopying, recording, or by any information storage and retrieval system, without permission in writing from the publisher.

Unless otherwise noted, Scripture quotations are taken from the *New Revised Standard Version of the Bible*, Anglicized Edition, copyright © 1989, 1995 by the Division of Christian Education of the National Council of the Churches of Christ in the USA. Used by permission. All rights reserved.

The extract marked NEB is from the *New English Bible*, copyright © The Delegates of the Oxford University Press and The Syndics of Cambridge University Press, 1961, 1970. Used by permission.

Every effort has been made to seek permission to use copyright material reproduced in this book. The publisher apologizes for those cases where permission might not have been sought and, if notified, will formally seek permission at the earliest opportunity.

Cover and book design by Mark Sullivan
Cover image © picjumbo.com

ISBN 978-1-63253-104-9

Copyright ©2016, Laurence Freeman. All rights reserved.
First published in Great Britain by SPCK.
First U.S. edition published by Franciscan Media, 2016.

Published by Franciscan Media
28 W. Liberty St.
Cincinnati, OH 45202
www.FranciscanMedia.org

Printed in the United States of America.
Printed on acid-free paper.
16 17 18 19 20 5 4 3 2 1

CONTENTS

INTRODUCTION

> He fasted for forty days and forty nights.
> —Matthew 4:2

Forty is one of those numbers that seem to turn up everywhere. It has many symbolic meanings but in biblical terms, as well as in the Asian traditions, it points to the idea of process, a time of trial or preparation during which people are made ready for the next stage in their development. The Hebrews spent forty years in the wilderness before entering their promised land; Jesus spent forty days fasting in the desert before beginning to teach publicly; Muhammad spent forty days fasting in a cave and the Buddha sat for the same length of time meditating under the bodhi tree. According to Kabbalah, it takes forty years to complete a cycle of transformation from intention to integration.

This book is a guide and, I hope, a friendly companion to an interior journey of forty days that you can make through the Christian period of Lent. It can also be a way of beginning to make the practice of meditation a part of your daily life.

Like the number forty, meditation is found in all the major religious traditions—not, however, as a symbolic idea but as a practice. What is meditation? First, it is truly simple and that is why it is universal. The truly universal is always simple. But that does not mean it is also easy. Young children find meditation entirely natural and they certainly enjoy it. Perhaps they don't find it easy, but because they approach it more as play (recreation), than as a solemn struggle or obligation, they can meditate, and choose to meditate. This means they experience the benefits and fruits of the practice very directly.

By "benefits" I mean things you can measure, like blood pressure, stress levels, sleep patterns and so on, all of which seem to be beneficially influenced by meditation. By "fruits" I mean things that you can't measure, but you are certainly aware of. These are even more important to the human and humane quality of life—things like love, joy, peace, patience, gentleness, kindness and self-control.

In recent years mindfulness training—a form of Buddhist practice adapted to the modern secular and scientific culture—has attracted much attention for the benefits it is claimed to bestow. Some skepticism is often raised at the scientific quality of these claims, but clearly people practice it because it makes them feel better.

Meditation is another step, however, even more simple and yet in a way more challenging, because of this more radical simplicity. In mindfulness techniques the attention remains on yourself (thoughts, feelings, sensations, body scan). In meditation the work is to take the attention off yourself. This is the simplest and hardest thing in the world to do and yet also the most transformative and liberating.

Meditation is a discipline and you will appreciate this for yourself as soon as you try it. The word *discipline* comes from the Latin *discere*, meaning "to learn." We need discipline of course in learning a language, a musical instrument, to drive a car or to love and stay in a relationship. Discipline is not helpful if it is imposed by an external force against our will (except perhaps when we are two years old). If it is to work, discipline needs to be freely accepted and followed. This is especially true of a spiritual discipline. And yet without discipline we remain locked under the control of our ego and its repertoire of fears, anxieties, fantasies and desires. We are free only when we can choose to say yes or no from a place of enlightened self-knowledge.

Meditation is a learning process and it is natural and useful to join up with others who are learning the same thing. Learning together makes the acquisition of new knowledge easier and quicker. In meditation the new knowledge is actually more of a *new way of knowing* rather than additional information. A new meditator told me that he knew the daily practice was working because his wife told him that he was easier to live with, and that he was paying her more attention; and also because, on his walk to work every morning, he discovered that he was noticing the world around him rather than, as before, being compulsively trapped in his own stressful plans and anxieties. Like many people learning to meditate he found it helpful to meditate with others on a regular basis, in person or even online.

Meditation is solitary—I can't meditate for you and you can't meditate for me. We have to take personal responsibility for learning it. But at the same time meditation is communal—it gives us both a real, and more deeply felt sense of relationship and interdependence.[1] In fact it is not exaggeration to say that meditation will make you a more loving person. However you perceive or describe it, the practice of meditation that this book can help you to start will lead to a change in you. So don't meditate if you don't want to change.

The forty days and nights of Lent are about simplification, purification, getting priorities reestablished and remembering that God, not my ego, is the centre of reality. Whatever discipline you take up for Lent (giving up sweets or alcohol, doing spiritual reading, spending more time with your loved ones, helping someone in need) it is about this—simplification and purification.

The ancient word for this discipline was *ascesis* and it was used as a metaphor from the training exercises of athletes. Lent is a time for spiritual ascesis or exercise, shedding some unnecessary mental fat, toning the muscles of attention and patience. This book can help you use the forty days to learn to meditate. If you do this you might find that what you learn will not end on Easter Sunday, but will stay with you and enrich your daily experience for the rest of your life's journey.

* * *

I have spoken above about meditation but haven't said yet how to do it. The way of meditation I would recommend is in many ways universal, but also an integral part of the Christian tradition of prayer. In this tradition it is called the "prayer of the heart." This distinguishes it from either mental prayer or the external forms of worship with which many Christians have come to identify prayer.

Prayer is like a wheel with many spokes. The different spokes represent different forms of prayer—these can be explicitly religious such as those we practice in church, or less obviously so, like walking, exercise, making music, or art. Whatever concentrates our attention in a selfless way can be said to be a form of prayer. The fruit of all prayer is a calmer mind and a more open and compassionate heart.

In this way of meditation—praying in the heart, or what Jesus calls the "inner room"—we are not speaking to God or thinking about God or asking God for things.[2] Meditation is not what you think. We are *being with* God.

The early Christian monks, the desert fathers and mothers, said that meditation was the "laying aside of thoughts." This means good and bad thoughts, silly as well as wise ones. In meditation we are not trying to have good or better thoughts. If you get an inspired solution to a problem you are troubled by, let it go and it should be there when you finish your meditation (although by then it may not feel so inspired!).[3]

Sit down with your back straight. You can use a straight-backed chair or a cushion or meditation bench. Sit alert and comfortably, so that you can sit still throughout the meditation. Close your eyes lightly. Begin to repeat a single word or mantra and try to repeat it continuously, faithfully throughout the period of the meditation. When thoughts, problems, plans, memories, fantasies, anxieties, whatever, rise in the mind let them go and return your attention to the mantra. I recommend the word *maranatha*. This is an ancient Christian prayer-word but also one that can be used by all, young and old, those with faith and those without. It means "Come, Lord" but we are not consciously thinking of its meaning while we repeat it. If you choose this word say it as four syllables: ma-ra-na-tha. Articulate it clearly in the mind and listen to it as you repeat it.

The simplicity and stillness of the mantra will lead you into the silence that is pure prayer. There is nothing so much like God as silence, according to Meister Eckhart. The simple discipline is to say the mantra from the beginning to the end of the meditation—as best you can. Don't evaluate yourself. The thought of failure is just another thought to lay aside.

Saying the mantra is the interior form of the discipline of meditation. Actually sitting down to it every day is the outer form. Early morning and early evening are the ideal times but we have to adapt to circumstances. In the morning try to meditate before you check your emails or listen to the news. You can read the Lenten reading for the day from this book after the meditation. In the evening, try not to leave the second meditation too late as you may find that the spirit is willing but the flesh is weak. You can also then reread the daily reading from the morning. In this way your meditation practice will help you to find a balance and stability in your daily life, whatever kind of day it has been.

A lot can happen in forty days and forty nights. More useful things will happen if we enter into this period of sweet discipline with open hearts and minds, with conscious attention. It's not about succeeding, however, but it's about simply being faithful. That's when the most interesting, enlivening things happen. It is then that our sense of God is opened, transforming everything.

—*Laurence Freeman, OSB*

How to Meditate

To meditate, begin with your physical posture. Sit down (chair, cushion on the floor or meditation bench). Keep your back straight. Relaxed and alert, sit still. Let go of any points of tension in your shoulders and face especially. Close your eyes lightly.

Then silently, interiorly and without moving your lips or tongue, begin to repeat a single word or phrase, sacred in your own faith tradition. Recommended for the Christian meditator is the Aramaic prayer phrase found in Scripture: *maranatha*. Repeat it faithfully. Say it gently without force or impatience. Four equal syllables: ma-ra-na-tha. Say it throughout the meditation period.

When you are distracted by thoughts, words or images drop the distraction and return to your mantra, from beginning to end. Let go of all your thoughts. Meditation is not what you think.

Aim at first to meditate for twenty minutes, twice a day—morning and evening, as far as possible. Gradually you can increase to thirty minutes. Time the session with a watch or timer.

Do the best you can. Failure teaches us wisdom. Let go of perfectionism and evaluation and instead be as faithful to the practice as you can be.

Meditating with others on a regular basis will help you develop your daily practice.

Starting to Meditate

Like everything new, meditation can seem strange at first. Allow time in your day to meditate and allow time to feel familiar with the experience. One day you will see how important meditation is to the quality of the meaning of your life—each day. For now, and the next six weeks, just do it.

Do the best you can (not less than your best), to meditate twice a day for twenty minutes. If you can only do it for five or ten minutes, start there. If you can only do it once a day, start there. But begin.

And remember you are in solitude when you meditate—only you can do it—but you are never less alone.

Try the best place to do it—bedroom, sitting-room, bathroom. Try the best time of the morning and evening. Begin.

ASH WEDNESDAY
Matthew 6:1–6, 16–18

"Beware of practicing your piety before others in order to be seen by them; for then you have no reward from your Father in heaven. So whenever you give alms, do not sound a trumpet before you, as the hypocrites do in the synagogues and in the streets, so that they may be praised by others. Truly I tell you, they have received their reward. But when you give alms, do not let your left hand know what your right hand is doing, so that your alms may be done in secret; and your Father who sees in secret will reward you. And whenever you pray, do not be like the hypocrites; for they love to stand and pray in the synagogues and at the street corners, so that they may be seen by others. Truly I tell you, they have received their reward. But whenever you pray, go into your room and shut the door and pray to your Father who is in secret; and your Father who sees in secret will reward you.... And whenever you fast, do not look dismal, like the hypocrites, for they disfigure their faces so as to show others that they are fasting. Truly I tell you, they have received their reward. But when you fast, put oil on your head and wash your face, so that your fasting may be seen not by others but by your Father who is in secret; and your Father who sees in secret will reward you."

DO NOT LET YOUR LEFT HAND KNOW WHAT YOUR RIGHT HAND IS DOING

Is the universe friendly? Einstein thought this was a major question for modern people. Spiritual intelligence says yes, and the sign of this is the way we are given second chances. The problem is in recognizing and believing them and not being depressed by the failure of the world to meet all our expectations on time. Lent, and meditation, offer a chance to press and keep your finger lightly on the reset button.

Liturgical time runs parallel to work time and relaxation time. Actually, when acknowledged ("Today I begin Lent") it runs through all time. And, in the next forty days, it can radiate and renew all our experience of time. Thus we arrive awake at the timeless moment of resurrection with a better chance of experiencing the power of its steady presence, today and throughout each day.

How can we make the best of this season? Commit more generously and absolutely to the twice-daily meditation. Also embrace two other realistic yet hope-filled practices to develop self-control as a way to personal liberty and freedom from anxiety, compulsiveness and fear. One should involve moderation and the other, exertion. Reduce (or drop) something you do excessively—like alcohol or time-wasting. Add something you don't do enough—like a daily nonjudgmental act of kindness to someone in need or simply being nice to people when they annoy you.

And read an appropriate Lenten Gospel—there are passages included here with each reflection. You could memorize the short verse from today's passage emphasized at the beginning of this reflection and recall it during the day. Let's enjoy a second chance to remain present, awake and simple that Lent gives us this year.

THURSDAY AFTER ASH WEDNESDAY
Luke 9:22–25

"The Son of Man must undergo great suffering, and be rejected by the elders, chief priests, and scribes, and be killed, and on the third day be raised." Then he said to them all, 'If any want to become my followers, let them deny themselves and take up their cross daily and follow me. For those who want to save their life will lose it, and those who lose their life for my sake will save it. What does it profit them if they gain the whole world, but lose or forfeit themselves?'"

THOSE WHO WANT TO SAVE THEIR LIFE WILL LOSE IT

The English poet George Herbert has been called the poet of the inner weather. Being English, he could talk a lot about the weather and was finely attuned to its lesser and greater variations. "After so many deaths I live and write / I once more smell the dew and rain / And relish versing."[4]

Our five senses and physical life are intricately woven into our spiritual seasons. When our spiritual life is clouded by negative states of mind or recurrent patterns that keep us self-absorbed, our senses too lose their edge. We feel dull, depressed and unengaged with the world and all its relationships, in which we live and breathe. But when we are spiritually awake, our senses pick up the vitality of life and we can smell, see, touch, hear and taste—whether it is ravishing or disgusting, at least we will sense it fully for what it is. The sensual part of our consciousness needs the spiritual and the spiritual needs the sensual.

When they are balanced they merge and form a single, perfect language and we experience wholeness.

So, as Lent gets underway, consider the two practices I described yesterday in the light of what you are sensing. Don't become too conceptual, too idealized about them. Each day you can evaluate how you have been doing but with detachment and humor rather than a judgmental attitude.

The morning and evening meditations calibrate all this in a way that is natural and spontaneous. Through them, you lose yourself wholly and find yourself in your wholeness. You don't have to keep looking under the hood of the car to examine the engine. You will feel that the car (rather like the ego) is running properly and getting you where you are going.

FRIDAY AFTER ASH WEDNESDAY
Matthew 9:14–15

"Then the disciples of John came to him, saying, "Why do we and the Pharisees fast often, but your disciples do not fast?" And Jesus said to them, "The wedding-guests cannot mourn as long as the bridegroom is with them, can they? The days will come when the bridegroom is taken away from them, and then they will fast."

THE WEDDING-GUESTS CANNOT MOURN AS LONG AS THE BRIDEGROOM IS WITH THEM, CAN THEY?

In a digital age virtual reality seems more convenient than actuality. Whims can be satisfied on the spot. You can pay extra for same-day delivery. If the name of an actor is on the tip of your tongue, Google can help your memory. When you want out-of-season vegetables you just need to find the right supermarket. In practice, these are perks of twenty-first-century living (in the First World) that we are reluctant to give up.

The incremental danger, however, is a creeping distance from the world where disappointment and loss are inevitable. We feel our human rights have been abused when it is merely our consumer desires that have been denied. Contentment becomes a superficial feeling that keeps us permanently vulnerable, disassociated and self-centered.

Jesus defended his disciples for not fasting while he was with them. He must have been a joyful and exhilarating person to be with. But he warned them of an impending separation and to be prepared for loss. There is a time-cycle for everything in life that even the best-stocked 24-hour convenience store cannot change.

Blake said, "Kiss the joy as it flies."[5] The practices of Lent, resting on the foundation of the meditating day, help us to be both realistic and happy. The two go together in a way that consumerism can never fathom.

Saturday after Ash Wednesday
Luke 5:27–32

"After this he went out and saw a tax-collector named Levi, sitting at the tax booth; and he said to him, "Follow me." And he got up, left everything, and followed him. Then Levi gave a great banquet for him in his house; and there was a large crowd of tax-collectors and others sitting at the table with them. The Pharisees and their scribes were complaining to his disciples, saying, "Why do you eat and drink with tax-collectors and sinners?" Jesus answered, "Those who are well have no need of a physician, but those who are sick; I have come to call not the righteous but sinners to repentance.""

I HAVE COME TO CALL NOT THE RIGHTEOUS BUT SINNERS TO REPENTANCE

After I had suffered years of traveling in misery, an airline sent me a thank you for clocking up so many miles and Gold Status for life. (I just mistyped "God status.") I am skeptical about their promises, but for the time being it makes check-in and waiting easier. The way the perk is offered is meant to make you feel special, but woe to those who fall for that temptation.

Special status is an illusion in which we take refuge when things are going well. We may even thank God because the storm missed us and hit the next peninsula. When things go badly—when we lose what we have enjoyed or fail to achieve what we have long worked and hoped for, or have the time of pleasure cut short—the special status feels as if it has been withdrawn. Imagine what the Jews in Nazi Germany felt as little by little their social and professional rights were whittled away and they were reduced in a short time to non-citizens. This was a nightmare of insecurity, which we all have, come true.

Even if it is just life and ever-changing circumstances that cause us to lose what we value—like health—we get a nagging feeling of being picked on. We feel angry at something (a Santa Claus God or the government). We feel we have lost status through illness or even when undergoing tests. There is a sense of superiority that the healthy and happy can hardly help feeling toward the sick and those whom life seems to have treated badly. Yet this sense of being separated and marginalized by fate has a grace. Jesus said he came for the sick, not the healthy. He dined with sinners, not church leaders. So who's "special"?

No wonder—when they see this—that sinners make the best contemplatives. We may also discover this truth as we progress in the practice of meditation.

WEEK ONE

Starting to Meditate

The past few days have been your initiation—self-invitation—into being a meditator. How did you do? What do you feel about it? What have you learned about yourself? Meditating is the fast track to self-knowledge. And it is self-knowledge that changes us the most.

You might be feeling a sense of non-achievement—maybe you haven't meditated as much as you intended or for as long. No problem. What has it taught you?

Don't judge your meditation by the degree of distraction you feel. But by your faithfulness and your ability to keep on beginning.

See the mantra (say the mantra) as a friend, not a task to perform perfectly. There are no perfect meditators. Only faithful ones. As you say the mantra, listen to it—don't visualize it. Say it with just enough effort to keep it as the focus of your attention. Don't try too hard. But don't give up. Experience is your teacher.

FIRST SUNDAY OF LENT
Mark 1:12–15

"And the Spirit immediately drove him out into the wilderness. He was in the wilderness for forty days, tempted by Satan; and he was with the wild beasts; and the angels waited on him. Now after John was arrested, Jesus came to Galilee, proclaiming the good news of God, and saying, 'The time is fulfilled, and the kingdom of God has come near; repent, and believe in the good news.'"

HE WAS WITH THE WILD BEASTS; AND THE ANGELS WAITED ON HIM

A little girl looked at me once when I was wearing my white habit and asked me, "Are you an angel?" When questions arise from a pure place—even if it is the mytho-magical mind of a six-year-old—they have an authentic force. When that period of development passes, the same questions become regressive or silly. So to look around for traces of angels' feathers, or imagine they are hovering behind you, as in cartoons, is missing the point. But it is a sad person who has never recognized the ministry of angels.

I don't know what angels really are. Perhaps they are autonomous forces in the psyche, waves of benevolence and compassion radiating as if they were messengers sent from the divine source of love and meeting us in our loneliest times of distress. Jesus was cared for after he was exhausted by what he went through in the forty days in the desert. He had confronted the dark forces of his ego, urging him to power, self-sufficiency and pride. He had seen through them and did not succumb to the temptation to give up the struggle to be real, to stay real and to deny the easy allurements of illusion. But that can be exhausting at times and, like any human being, he needed to be ministered to.

Where do we find this ministry of spiritual friendship and accompaniment in our own lives? Not perhaps in hosts of angels flying down from above, but in the sharing of the pilgrimage ever deeper into the realm of the real. Although the commitment to reality—which is also what our daily meditation signifies—demands solitude, it also opens us up to community. The people we meet in the desert of our solitude are real friends. We recognize each other and value each other but also know we cannot possess each other because the pilgrimage is also a journey into a dispossession of our own selves.

Monday
Matthew 25:31–36

"When the Son of Man comes in his glory, and all the angels with him, then he will sit on the throne of his glory. All the nations will be gathered before him, and he will separate people one from another as a shepherd separates the sheep from the goats, and he will put the sheep at his right hand and the goats at the left. Then the king will say to those at his right hand, 'Come, you that are blessed by my Father, inherit the kingdom prepared for you from the foundation of the world; for I was hungry and you gave me food, I was thirsty and you gave me something to drink, I was a stranger and you welcomed me, I was naked and you gave me clothing, I was sick and you took care of me, I was in prison and you visited me.'"

I WAS THIRSTY AND YOU GAVE ME SOMETHING TO DRINK, I WAS A STRANGER AND YOU WELCOMED ME

Can you teach compassion? Can you regulate it? After some shocking, almost unbelievable cases of brutality in care institutions toward the defenseless and the elderly, training courses and tighter rules were introduced. Somebody was doing something. (After a disaster we say, "somebody should do something about it.")

Perhaps training and regulations help enforce the basic principle that at the least we should do no harm to others. But compassion is more than behavior. It is the way that things are done, the fundamental current through which action flows toward self and others. And the source of compassion is not less than the true self, that irreducible "I" in which the ego has been fully absorbed and therefore is invisible and casts no shadow.

When action flows from this non-geographical point of pure identity, it is unconcerned about what it looks like and even about whether it is good or bad in the eyes of others. Compassion is pure action issuing from purity of heart. It is carried along toward others by a force of generosity that is too complete, and too fulfilling for it to worry about what it is going to get in return.

Does this sound like meditation? It does, because it is meditation. When the true self is in play, everything that is thought and done is a form of meditation. Until then, we have to learn and relearn to stay centered and be simple. We have to remember when we forget. Saying the mantra is just this learning process. To say the mantra wholeheartedly, generously, purely, begins to orientate the whole person in a direction that is no longer self-centered. It sets this tone for everything. Meditation lets us be compassionate because it is compassionate.

TUESDAY
Matthew 6:7–15

"When you are praying, do not heap up empty phrases as the Gentiles do; for they think that they will be heard because of their many words. Do not be like them, for your Father knows what you need before you ask him. Pray then in this way: Our Father in heaven, hallowed be your name. Your kingdom come. Your will be done, on earth as it is in heaven. Give us this day our daily bread. And forgive us our debts, as we also have forgiven our debtors. And do not bring us to the time of trial, but rescue us from the evil one. For if you forgive others their trespasses, your heavenly Father will also forgive you; but if you do not forgive others, neither will your Father forgive your trespasses."

OUR FATHER IN HEAVEN

The drops of water that hang suspended precariously on the underside of a thin branch of a bare tree are a closer image of God than the pictures we concoct of thrones or sanctuaries or leather chairs in the CEO's office.

Why do we want to make God such a powerful force that works (as we like to imagine) by intervening and controlling situations and making things turn out comfortably for his favorites? We imagine our Father in heaven to be sitting on such a mighty throne, because heaven is like the first-class lounge, the fast-track lane, the exclusive club. You expect to find the best furniture in such places. Such an imagined, projected God will ever be inaccessible and unknowable because—like the rich, the famous, and all the power-brokers of this world—he must be worshipped, feared, and flattered from the unbridgeable distance set up between the ordinary and the divine.

But what if the true nature and "power" of God was expressed in quite different human metaphors? What if heaven was a place where there were no social distinctions, where the vulnerable was more powerful than the oppressive? Fragility, tenderness, the marginal, the simply beautiful rather than the magnificent? These are much more difficult to believe as symbols of what "God," the verb, and "heaven," the non-spatial place, mean. Yet they speak to us with greater truth and leave a deeper impression. They bring us closer to seeing what the truth is by helping us to see things as they truly are in a world where we habitually weave illusions of success to conceal our fears and insecurities.

In a day balanced on the twin levers of morning and evening meditation, the strong, true subtleties of life win out over the habits of fantasy. In Lenten days when the spirit of self-control and careful attention to detail sharpen our perception and soften our anxiety, God and heaven come down to earth.

WEDNESDAY
Luke 11:28–32

"But he said, 'Blessed rather are those who hear the word of God and obey it!' When the crowds were increasing, he began to say, 'This generation is an evil generation; it asks for a sign, but no sign will be given to it except the sign of Jonah. For just as Jonah became a sign to the people of Nineveh, so the Son of Man will be to this generation. The queen of the South will rise at the judgement with the people of this generation and condemn them, because she came from the ends of the earth to listen to the wisdom of Solomon, and see, something greater than Solomon is here! The people of Nineveh will rise up at the judgment with this generation and condemn it, because they repented at the proclamation of Jonah, and see, something greater than Jonah is here!'"

THEY REPENTED AT THE PROCLAMATION OF JONAH, AND SEE,
SOMETHING GREATER THAN JONAH IS HERE

It's hard to change your mind (the real meaning of repent) when you have it made up. We often dig our heels in and resist, just to avoid changing plans or ways of perception. Some people are temperamentally almost impossible to budge once they have decided on a course of action, because they can so easily rely on their plans to give a sense of control and safety. To change a small thing makes them feel insecure about many things and even sends warning signals down deep into the caverns where their fear of death lurks.

When it comes to our character or personality, as shaped by years of experience, it seems even more difficult to effect change. For a long time, this was scientifically justified by the conviction that the brain itself could not change much after childhood. We were set for life after a relatively young age. But now neurobiology has discovered that the brain's plasticity is, remarkably, youthfully adaptive long into our life-journey.

So there's no excuse. Jonah was a prophet (born not far from Nazareth) and Jesus referred to him to illustrate how, once again, the minds of people were refusing to open (the precondition for change) to what a prophet had to show them. We have all kinds of means to resist changing our mind—denial, aggression, and procrastination being among the favorites.

To change or repent means not only the content of our beliefs and ideas, but the actual mode of perception by which consciousness operates. Saying the mantra in our daily Lenten practice tricks us out of these resistances and fears by first affecting the quality of awareness through seeing what is really there. Then behavior changes. Then thoughts. Radical change without force. Radical simplicity with unbounded love, in daily increments. The meaning of *repentance*.

THURSDAY
Matthew 7:7–12

"Ask, and it will be given to you; search, and you will find; knock, and the door will be opened for you. For everyone who asks receives, and everyone who searches finds, and for everyone who knocks, the door will be opened. Is there anyone among you who, if your child asks for bread, will give a stone? Or if the child asks for a fish, will give a snake? If you then, who are evil, know how to give good gifts to your children, how much more will your Father in heaven give good things to those who ask him! In everything do to others as you would have them do to you; for this is the law and the prophets."

ASK, AND IT WILL BE GIVEN TO YOU; SEARCH, AND YOU WILL FIND; KNOCK, AND THE DOOR WILL BE OPENED FOR YOU

There must be a catch.

Of course there is, stupid. Do you think God, the universe, whatever, is going to give you what you want, when and how you order it, like a home delivery? Is God a pizza boy?

No, of course not. But he said (and he's the Son of God, right?) that you only have to ask and you will receive. Well, this is what I'd like to ask for; and it's really not as selfish as it sounds. I'm not stupid by the way. I am trying to have faith. If I get what I ask for I will be a really happy person and then it will be easy to be generous and nice to others. I've thought about this a lot—no, not fantasized, really thought. I know what will make me a good person. These are just the basic requirements.

Tell me, then.

They sound a bit this-worldly, I agree.

Go on then.

Well, I'll whisper it to you. This is what I'd like to ask for... (whispers).

I can understand that. My wish-list would be much the same. Not extravagant. Material and emotional security, good health, and a nice home in which to enjoy it all.

More or less, yes. But I could do so much good in the world if I had that.

Well, it's not impossible you will get that—even for a few decades if you're lucky. But you know you asked, "Is there a catch?"

Yes.

Here it is: Whatever you wish that others would do to you, do so to them.

Now? Even before I get the delivery?

You said it.

Yeah, and meditation twice a day, right?

Yes, that would help you with your reading of Scripture.

FRIDAY
Matthew 5:20–26

"For I tell you, unless your righteousness exceeds that of the scribes and Pharisees, you will never enter the kingdom of heaven. You have heard that it was said to those of ancient times, 'You shall not murder'; and 'whoever murders shall be liable to judgment.' But I say to you that if you are angry with a brother or sister, you will be liable to judgment; and if you insult a brother or sister, you will be liable to the council; and if you say, 'You fool,' you will be liable to the hell of fire. So when you are offering your gift at the altar, if you remember that your brother or sister has something against you, leave your gift there before the altar and go; first be reconciled to your brother or sister, and then come and offer your gift. Come to terms quickly with your accuser while you are on the way to court with him, or your accuser may hand you over to the judge, and the judge to the guard, and you will be thrown into prison. Truly I tell you, you will never get out until you have paid the last penny."

FIRST BE RECONCILED TO YOUR BROTHER OR SISTER

At the Good Heart Seminar when the Dalai Lama was commenting on the Gospels, Sr. Eileen O'Hea asked him: "Your holiness, would you like to meet Jesus and if so what question would you ask him?" Without pause he responded, "Yes, I would like to, and I would ask him, 'What is the nature of the Father?'"

In the light of today's Gospel they would probably get on very well if they did meet. The Dalai Lama's question—one that few Christians ever think about—goes to the heart of Christian faith and the profound nature of Jesus. With that foundation, their common understanding of the nature of religion, which today's Gospel teaching illustrates, would be in perfect harmony.

The Dalai Lama has said: "My simple religion is kindness. There is no need for temples; no need for complicated philosophy. Our own brain, our own heart is our temple; the philosophy is kindness." This might sound as if religion as a system of practices, rituals and beliefs has been or could be made redundant. If only. Humanity tried twice in the twentieth century and failed disastrously, as much so as if it had tried to abolish art or science. In the twenty-first century we have to renew religion, not abolish it.

But one day in the holy city (as the book of Revelation says), there will indeed be no temple "for its temple is the Lord God the Almighty and the Lamb" (Revelation 21:22). Until that happy day we have to listen to Jesus who speaks in tune with all religious leaders worth listening to; don't enter a church, temple, mosque, or synagogue unless you are prepared to love your enemies.

SATURDAY
Matthew 5:43–48

"You have heard that it was said, 'You shall love your neighbor and hate your enemy.' But I say to you, Love your enemies and pray for those who persecute you, so that you may be children of your Father in heaven; for he makes his sun rise on the evil and on the good, and sends rain on the righteous and on the unrighteous. For if you love those who love you, what reward do you have? Do not even the tax-collectors do the same? And if you greet only your brothers and sisters, what more are you doing than others? Do not even the Gentiles do the same? Be perfect, therefore, as your heavenly Father is perfect."

BE PERFECT, THEREFORE, AS YOUR HEAVENLY FATHER IS PERFECT

Get this and you get the whole Gospel and it changes your life. Fail to get it and the Gospel goes in one ear and out the other and your life is stuck in a repetitious cycle.

The key is understanding the word *perfect*. Seeing it to mean that we are flawless both condemns us (to continuous failure and second-ratedness), and lets us off the hook (there's no point in striving for the impossible). To make some more sense of it, let's see what other meanings there are for the word that in English is translated as "perfect."

The corresponding Greek word is *teleios*. It definitely does not mean the same as something we buy secondhand but which claims to be "in perfect condition" or a morally perfect person who has never, or will never make a mistake. Similarly, the

Hebrew word *tamim* does *not* intend to mean this unachievable, left-brain, almost abstract infallibility. Woe to those who think they are in this way perfect. They are perfect fools.

Both the Greek and Hebrew words would be better translated as "wholeness," "soundness," "integrity." The Latin *perfectus* also means something "fully developed," "completed." As in ordinary language the phrase "perfect stranger" doesn't describe someone who is ethically flawless, but someone completely unknown.

Perfection means not that we have not failed or won't do so again but that we know what wholeness, integrity and completeness mean. Plato said that the perfect (*teleios*) person is one who sees and is turned toward what is Good. That's half of perfection. What Jesus says here guides us to that point. The other half is keeping moving into that condition, that place of personal experience, through continual and dedicated effort.

There is a big, humbling gap here, of course, that is bridged by the other element of the Gospel teaching, which is forgiveness. When we think of it like this, forgiveness obviously has to begin with forgiving ourselves. And hatred, rejection and condemnation (mutations of true religion) begin with the self-righteous accusing of others, in the self-deceiving conviction that we haven't ourselves fallen short, or won't do so again.

St. James says perfection can be recognized in the way we control our tongue—our most unruly member—and harmonize our thoughts and our speech, our mind and heart. There is a big gap here too, day by day, and the bridge is conscious silence.

(Sounds like meditation perhaps?)

Still Starting to Meditate

If you have been meditating regularly, you may have begun to see some of the benefits. How would you describe these—a deeper, inner peace or stillness? A greater clarity of mind? A better quality of attention to those you live or work with? A deeper resonance with your mind and the Scriptures, and the mind of Christ? I don't want to put words in your mouth or thoughts in your head. What difference does meditation make? Some people say they can't express it, but they feel it. Maybe it's not experiences, rather a new kind of experience of enlarged awareness.

How are you doing with the twice-a-day challenge? How about the twenty minutes? Are you feeling that a good discipline is growing? Reflect on your physical posture and physical stillness. The stillness of body reflects and develops the stillness of mind.

"Be still and know that I am God." Paying attention to the mantra is the direct route to that stillness of total attention.

SECOND SUNDAY OF LENT
Mark 9:2–10

"Six days later, Jesus took with him Peter and James and John, and led them up a high mountain apart, by themselves. And he was transfigured before them, and his clothes became dazzling white, such as no one on earth could bleach them. And there appeared to them Elijah with Moses, who were talking with Jesus. Then Peter said to Jesus, 'Rabbi, it is good for us to be here; let us make three dwellings, one for you, one for Moses, and one for Elijah.' He did not know what to say, for they were terrified. Then a cloud overshadowed them, and from the cloud there came a voice, 'This is my Son, the Beloved; listen to him!' Suddenly when they looked around, they saw no one with them any more, but only Jesus. As they were coming down the mountain, he ordered them to tell no one about what they had seen, until after the Son of Man had risen from the dead. So they kept the matter to themselves, questioning what this rising from the dead could mean."

JESUS...LED THEM UP A HIGH MOUNTAIN APART, BY
THEMSELVES. AND HE WAS TRANSFIGURED BEFORE THEM

The great—and difficult—novelist Henry James was once taken to a Punch and Judy show by some mischievous friends. They were astounded at how totally absorbed he became in this very simple form of theater. After the performance he was very silent until they asked him what he had thought of it. "What an economy of means," he answered, and added wistfully, "what an economy of ends."

You could say the same of the Gospel and all its stories, like today's account of how Jesus was transfigured in light before the few close disciples he took with him up the mountain. The account is very spare (an economy of means) and the meaning is so simple that it defies an easy explanation (an economy of ends). When the Dalai Lama commented on this, he didn't describe it metaphorically but spoke of it as an example of what Tibetan thought calls the subtle—or "rainbow"—body.

Truth usually has this economy. We tend to diverge from the truth the more we analyze, complicate and define. We usually speak too much about things we don't understand but much less about things whose truth we really feel. This is why meditation is so economical, cutting out the waste of thoughts and words in the work of silence and getting directly to the simple end.

In the Transfiguration story, Peter (typically) got it wrong by talking, but without knowing what he was saying because "they were terrified." Why does the truth—and the simplicity that is the medium of truth—scare us so much? Why is silence (the letting go of thoughts) so challenging? Why is it hard to say the mantra faithfully? Why do the simple disciplines of Lent that we started recently often seem too much? Is it because we find it too simple to harmonize the means and the ends in a way that brings us to ourselves in the radiant glory of the present?

MONDAY
Luke 6:36–38

"Be merciful, just as your Father is merciful. Do not judge, and you will not be judged; do not condemn, and you will not be condemned. Forgive, and you will be forgiven; give, and it will be given to you. A good measure, pressed down, shaken together, running over, will be put into your lap; for the measure you give will be the measure you get back."

GIVE, AND IT WILL BE GIVEN TO YOU.
A GOOD MEASURE, PRESSED DOWN, SHAKEN TOGETHER,
RUNNING OVER, WILL BE PUT INTO YOUR LAP

This is morality 101, a variation on the golden rule of all wisdom traditions—do to others what you would like them to do to you. This would guarantee a just world and therefore an essentially peaceful one. As a moralist, Jesus is exact and exacting, but not so original.

The news recently has depressed us with more of the familiar stories of greedy, dishonest bankers and hypocritical politicians out for themselves. We expect them, if not to be better than we are, at least to be better in getting away with it or just keeping their voracious greed under some measure of control. They lack basic morality and decency by trying to get the "good measure" of Jesus's phrase without giving in the same measure. They can hardly be surprised for being named and shamed, though we who do so should examine the plank in our eye before we judge and condemn. It's hard for any of us, after all, to stop guzzling once we have started. Are we condemning the principle of the thing or the scale of it? I have a bowl of popcorn beside me as I write and can verify this.

But in today's teaching, the master is also revealing the mystical heart of morality. It is why Vaclav Havel spoke of the need for transcendence in the postmodern world. As we have now moved on from the postmodern, we might link it to the need for the mystical in a secular society. We need it simply because it's there and we can't be satisfied with leaving the truth suppressed.

Morality says to do to others what you want done to you. This can lead to saying that if that doesn't happen, then it's an eye for an eye. So we need to see the mystical, the transcendent underlying the moral; justice tempered with mercy. Learning to meditate, as you may be discovering, is a journey into the mystical depth of morality.

It's here in the expression about the good measure "running over [that] will be put into your lap." It is a measure that cannot be measured because it spills over the container into which it is being poured. Transcendence. The mystery of the altruistic gift of genuine generosity. Not earned income, not harvested produce, not accidental or merely cause and effect. What pours?

And not into your cosmic karma account. Into your lap.

(Yes, the bowl is empty.)

TUESDAY
Matthew 23:1–12

"Then Jesus said to the crowds and to his disciples, 'The scribes and the Pharisees sit on Moses' seat; therefore, do whatever they teach you and follow it; but do not do as they do, for they do not practice what they teach. They tie up heavy burdens, hard to bear, and lay them on the shoulders of others; but they themselves are unwilling to lift a finger to move them. They do all their deeds to be seen by others; for they make their phylacteries broad and their fringes long. They love to have the place of honor at banquets and the best seats in the synagogues, and to be greeted with respect in the marketplaces, and to have people call them rabbi. But you are not to be called rabbi, for you have one teacher, and you are all students. And call no one your father on earth, for you have one Father—the one in heaven. Nor are you to be called instructors, for you have one instructor, the Messiah. The greatest among you will be your servant. All who exalt themselves will be humbled, and all who humble themselves will be exalted.'"

THEREFORE DO WHATEVER THEY TEACH YOU
AND FOLLOW IT; BUT DO NOT DO AS THEY DO,
FOR THEY DO NOT PRACTICE WHAT THEY TEACH

Read the whole of the Gospel passage to get the full story of the excoriation of Jesus attacking the "Pharisees"—meaning the Muslim Pharisees, the Hindu Pharisees, the Israeli Pharisees, the secular Pharisees and, not least, the Christian Pharisees. Not many people can get away with this kind of exposure and condemnation of hypocrisy and exploitation. And, as we will see in Holy Week, Jesus didn't get away with it either. But we trust him, because of his suffering and its transcendent aftermath, and because he spoke from a passionate addiction to truth that is the only kind of addiction that sets us free.

Religion itself is laid bare here, not just one denomination. The corruption of the best is the worst, and so deserves the highest level of exposure and condemnation. Jesus then draws the logical conclusion: you are not to be called rabbi, for you have one teacher, and you are all brethren. Enter Luther and, a little later, the Second Vatican Council and then Pope Francis. Enter also the great Christian shadow, the anti-Christ (anti-Krishna, anti-Moses, anti-Muhammad, anti-everything authentic). You are all brothers and sisters—how are we going to square that uneconomic idealism with the need for hierarchy and privilege masquerading as service and humility? Easy: older brothers and inferior sisters.

Jesus is so radically disruptive. How can we domesticate him, how can the Church put a spin on this disturbing so-called 'good' news that turns the world as we know it—and our minds as we use them—upside down? That's easy too. Create systems that have the labels of truth but not the healing touch of the truth. Then idolize the systems.

How can we resist this inevitable tendency to the counter-revolutionary? If you don't know yet, let's pray this Lent will teach you as you learn how radical meditation really is.

WEDNESDAY
Matthew 20:17–28

"While Jesus was going up to Jerusalem, he took the twelve disciples aside by themselves, and said to them on the way, 'See, we are going up to Jerusalem, and the Son of Man will be handed over to the chief priests and scribes, and they will condemn him to death; then they will hand him over to the Gentiles to be mocked and flogged and crucified; and on the third day he will be raised.' Then the mother of the sons of Zebedee came to him with her sons, and kneeling before him, she asked a favour of him. And he said to her, 'What do you want?' She said to him, 'Declare that these two sons of mine will sit, one at your right hand and one at your left, in your kingdom.' But Jesus answered, 'You do not know what you are asking. Are you able to drink the cup that I am about to drink?' They said to him, 'We are able.' He said to them, 'You will indeed drink my cup, but to sit at my right hand and at my left, this is not mine to grant, but it is for those for whom it has been prepared by my Father.' When the ten heard it, they were angry with the two brothers. But Jesus called them to him and said, 'You know that the rulers of the Gentiles lord it over them, and their great ones are tyrants over them. It will not be so among you; but whoever wishes to be great among you must be your servant, and whoever wishes to be first among you must be your slave; just as the Son of Man came not to be served but to serve, and to give his life as a ransom for many.'"

THE SON OF MAN CAME NOT TO BE SERVED BUT TO SERVE, AND TO GIVE HIS LIFE AS A RANSOM FOR MANY

It's amazing how the Church can repeat these words of Jesus (read the whole Gospel passage and its total inversion of the social power-system) from a place of hierarchy and privilege. The only thing that exonerates the Church is the presence of people within the system (monks not included) who are well and painfully aware of this inconsistency. Who can blame people for leaving the institution? More, anyway, than can praise the people who stay in it and listen, really listen, to the words of the Master and suffer the cognitive dissonance.

In a recent interview with my friend Anne McDonnell, she spoke about her terminal illness and her experience of the present, and of the presence that emerges when we enter the present. Her Christian meditation centre near Norwich, England (Nogg's Barn), is one of the non-Googleable points on the planet where the truth is being lived. I loved—and I learned from—her speaking about the "hints of immortality in meditation," which she (understandably) found "difficult to talk about." Her words are teaching without the self-consciousness of the teacher.

The spirit of service and the true humility, which is the mystical–moral core of the Gospel, is inevitably linked to the knowledge of mortality. In meditation as well as in the lessons of life, mortality and immortality totally invert the power structures that Jesus is exposing.

If you haven't yet seen this aspect of Lent, I hope you do soon.

THURSDAY
Luke 16:19–31

"There was a rich man who was dressed in purple and fine linen and who feasted sumptuously every day. And at his gate lay a poor man named Lazarus, covered with sores, who longed to satisfy his hunger with what fell from the rich man's table; even the dogs would come and lick his sores. The poor man died and was carried away by the angels to be with Abraham. The rich man also died and was buried. In Hades, where he was being tormented, he looked up and saw Abraham far away with Lazarus by his side. He called out, 'Father Abraham, have mercy on me, and send Lazarus to dip the tip of his finger in water and cool my tongue; for I am in agony in these flames.' But Abraham said, 'Child, remember that during your lifetime you received your good things, and Lazarus in like manner evil things; but now he is comforted here, and you are in agony. Besides all this, between you and us a great chasm has been fixed, so that those who might want to pass from here to you cannot do so, and no one can cross from there to us.' He said, "Then, father, I beg you to send him to my father's house—for I have five brothers—that he may warn them, so that they will not also come into this place of torment." Abraham replied, "They have Moses and the prophets; they should listen to them." He said, 'No, father Abraham; but if someone goes to them from the dead, they will repent.' He said to him, 'If they do not listen to Moses and the prophets, neither will they be convinced even if someone rises from the dead.'"

BETWEEN YOU AND US A GREAT CHASM HAS BEEN FIXED

We live continuously with this chasm between the haves and the have-nots, the healthy and the sick, the smart and the dull, the gorgeous and the ugly, the slim and the fat, the lucky and the cursed. It's what we mean by "the world." Jesus said, 'The poor you will always have with you.' We will always fall somewhat short of perfect justice, because life itself is not fair and usually the fittest survive. The question is how deep and wide this chasm should be allowed to become. The wider it is, the more unreal we become; the deeper, the more painful is the chasm.

Today's parable is about the rich man (unnamed) and the poor man (Lazarus). When they die the rich man pays for his lack of compassion by going to a place of torment while Lazarus is taken by angels to Abraham's bosom. This seems simple justice but the wisdom of the Gospel is never simplistic. Lazarus does not speak. Abraham is his spokesman. The rich man, however, speaks. First he cries out for some relief like one of Dante's souls in the *Inferno*. Abraham says the chasm is now too wide to reach across. If we don't work now to narrow the gap between the rich and the poor it will increase exponentially and we will be irreparably divided.

But, in Gospel wisdom, the end is always a beginning. The rich man asks Abraham to warn his family about his fate, which they will also suffer if they do not change. Here is a change of heart, in the hard of heart. True, it's only for his own family that he is concerned so far, but it is still the beginning of compassion, of active concern for the needs of others. When the spring of compassion is released, the human chasm, the ego, the isolated self, is reconnected. In reconnection (the literal meaning of the word *religion*), the great healing happens. Meditation helps us make connections. It moves us into this change of heart. It is our ego that isolates us, not solitude.

FRIDAY
Matthew 21:33–46

"Listen to another parable. There was a landowner who planted a vineyard, put a fence around it, dug a wine press in it, and built a watchtower. Then he leased it to tenants and went to another country. When the harvest time had come, he sent his slaves to the tenants to collect his produce. But the tenants seized his slaves and beat one, killed another, and stoned another. Again he sent other slaves, more than the first; and they treated them in the same way. Finally he sent his son to them, saying, 'They will respect my son.' But when the tenants saw the son, they said to themselves, 'This is the heir; come, let us kill him and get his inheritance.' So they seized him, threw him out of the vineyard, and killed him. Now when the owner of the vineyard comes, what will he do to those tenants?' They said to him, 'He will put those wretches to a miserable death, and lease the vineyard to other tenants who will give him the produce at the harvest time.' Jesus said to them, 'Have you never read in the scriptures: "The stone that the builders rejected has become the cornerstone; this was the Lord's doing, and it is amazing in our eyes"? Therefore I tell you, the kingdom of God will be taken away from you and given to a people that produces the fruits of the kingdom. The one who falls on this stone will be broken to pieces; and it will crush anyone on whom it falls.' When the chief priests and the Pharisees heard his parables, they realized that he was speaking about them. They wanted to arrest him, but they feared the crowds, because they regarded him as a prophet."

The stone that the builders rejected has become the cornerstone

The ecological dream is to produce new energy by reprocessing all waste. Whatever has been thrown away or rejected is then reintegrated into the economy of life and a sense of equanimity and balance is achieved. But this is as hard to do in the inner life as at the global level.

Whenever something is thrown away (waste) or labeled as useless (rejected), there is an accompanying feeling of failure, or of a missed opportunity, or of incompleteness. The deepest human instinct is for meaning, wholeness, connection and integration. Nothing should ever be seen as separated from the whole simply because it can't be separate. We all have memories or relationships that we want to exclude because they don't fit in with the desired pattern of our life. "Don't dwell on the past" is good advice; but to reject the past before it has been integrated means it cannot be transcended. To reject, to repress, is merely to dig a deeper hole from which it becomes harder and harder to extricate ourselves. We may, in old age, forget what we repressed, but the past has not forgotten us.

Meditation is the exposure of our whole person to the radiance of the present. The stronger the light of the now, which contains all time and reveals the simple unity of life, the more this integration and subsequent transcendence occurs naturally, in its own good time. Many people have experienced this in moments of grace, or crisis, when time's structures (past, present, future) simply melt down, and they perceive the whole spectrum of a life-history in a moment. Contemplation is always contemporary.

Another way for what has been rejected to return (the "return of the repressed") is to realize that rejection never works. It only entangles us more with those aspects of a memory we dislike. Eventually it returns (as the rejected Jesus did) and is seen very differently.

An illness which throws life into a skid where all control is lost becomes a revelation and a blessing. A handicapped child seen as an inconvenience, a punishment or a shame can be rejected in various ways; then the family's eyes are opened and they see the child as a gift of God that floods them with wonder and gratitude. The rejected stone becomes the foundation stone.

SATURDAY
Luke 15:1–3, 11–32

"Now all the tax-collectors and sinners were coming near to listen to him. And the Pharisees and the scribes were grumbling and saying, 'This fellow welcomes sinners and eats with them.' So he told them this parable:… 'There was a man who had two sons. The younger of them said to his father, "Father, give me the share of the property that will belong to me." So he divided his property between them. A few days later the younger son gathered all he had and travelled to a distant country, and there he squandered his property in dissolute living. When he had spent everything, a severe famine took place throughout that country, and he began to be in need. So he went and hired himself out to one of the citizens of that country, who sent him to his fields to feed the pigs. He would gladly have filled himself with the pods that the pigs were eating; and no one gave him anything. But when he came to himself he said, "How many of my father's hired hands have bread enough and to spare, but here I am dying of hunger! I will get up and go to my father, and I will say to him, 'Father, I have sinned against heaven and before you; I am no longer worthy to be called your son; treat me like one of your hired hands.'" So he set off and went to his father. But while he was still far off, his father saw him and was filled with compassion; he ran and put his arms around him and kissed him. Then the son said to him, "Father, I have sinned against heaven and before you; I am no longer worthy to be called your son." But the father said to his slaves, "Quickly, bring out a robe—the best one—and put it on him; put a ring on his finger and sandals on his feet. And get the fatted calf and kill it, and let us eat and celebrate; for this son of mine was dead and is alive again; he was lost and is found!" And they began to celebrate. Now his elder son was in the field; and when he came and approached the house, he heard music and dancing. He called one of the slaves and asked what was going on. He replied, "Your brother has come, and your father has killed the fatted calf, because he has got him back safe and sound." Then he became angry and refused to go in. His father came out and began to plead with him. But he answered his father, "Listen! For all these years I have been working like a slave for you, and I have never disobeyed your command; yet you have never given me even a young goat so that I might celebrate with my friends. But when this son of yours came back, who has devoured your property with prostitutes, you killed the fatted calf for him!" Then the father said to him, "Son, you are always with me, and all that is mine is yours. But we had to celebrate and rejoice, because this brother of yours was dead and has come to life; he was lost and has been found."'"

THIS FELLOW WELCOMES SINNERS AND EATS WITH THEM
Rather like Pope Francis, Jesus got more understanding and support from outside the religious establishment than from within it. But that is true of most radical thinkers and reformers. Those outside can better understand the essential simplicity of the reformers' mission; and to simplify complex power systems is bound to make you enemies.

The parable Jesus gave in response to this carping comment about him associating with sinners is that of the prodigal son. Once again it shows how moral vision derives from a mystical experience. In our work of teaching meditation to, for example, business school students, this is the implicit rationale. Meditation leads us into experience because it naturally awakens all experience so that ethical dilemmas become more easily understood and solved. Experience is a stronger persuader than argument, and we act well to the degree that we see clearly.

The parable (better called the parable of the two brothers) has an obvious moral point. Don't condemn the wrongdoer once he or she has begun to change. Encourage rehabilitation by affirmation, forgiveness, and acceptance, just as the father gives a party for his returning black sheep. Given the two brothers' personalities, which seems closer to the father? They are in fact equidistant. The prodigal brother slunk home expecting to be rebuked and can't understand the nature of the father's expansive love. The older, killjoy brother is entirely lacking in the generosity that characterizes his father. They are the two faces of the ego in all of us: the one part that wants to run after pleasure and the other that likes to take the moral high ground and feel justified in condemnation.

How much they misread the father, our true self. In the symbolism of his joy, his abandonment of self-importance, and his sheer exuberance of love we see the transcendent, mystical dimension underpinning the moral. Without knowledge of this essential truth of the joy of being and the unconditional nature of love, the ego will prevail.

Each time we meditate, we are like the prodigal returning home to be embraced and also like the older brother learning that being good is more than doing good. Lent is a time when, by simplifying selected aspects of our lives and strengthening our discipline where it is weak, we can see ourselves in each of these three characters and decide—is it so difficult?—which one we want to be.

Starting Again to Meditate

Meditation brings benefits you can measure: cardiovascular; and perceive objectively: a better sleeping pattern, greater patience. Have you noticed any of these? Or have they been pointed out to you by people you live or work with? Behind these effects lies the work of attention. Attention is the heart of prayer—indeed, of all human relationships.

Your productive work of attention is your saying the mantra. So don't worry about distractions—they only give you the opportunity to say your mantra more faithfully. Let the thoughts come and go. Keep your focus on the mantra, which at times seems like a windshield wiper working in a storm.

Have you developed your daily rhythm, and perhaps a personal routine or ritual around your times of meditation? Do you notice if the morning or evening meditation is easier? More importantly, can you sense that good work is being done in you, even if it is hard going?

THIRD SUNDAY OF LENT
John 2:13–25

"The Passover of the Jews was near, and Jesus went up to Jerusalem. In the temple he found people selling cattle, sheep, and doves, and the money-changers seated at their tables. Making a whip of cords, he drove all of them out of the temple, both the sheep and the cattle. He also poured out the coins of the money-changers and overturned their tables. He told those who were selling the doves, 'Take these things out of here! Stop making my Father's house a market-place!' His disciples remembered that it was written, 'Zeal for your house will consume me.' The Jews then said to him, 'What sign can you show us for doing this?' Jesus answered them, 'Destroy this temple, and in three days I will raise it up.' The Jews then said, 'This temple has been under construction for forty-six years, and will you raise it up in three days?' But he was speaking of the temple of his body. After he was raised from the dead, his disciples remembered that he had said this; and they believed the scripture and the word that Jesus had spoken. When he was in Jerusalem during the Passover festival, many believed in his name because they saw the signs that he was doing. But Jesus on his part would not entrust himself to them, because he knew all people and needed no one to testify about anyone; for he himself knew what was in everyone."

BUT JESUS ON HIS PART WOULD NOT ENTRUST HIMSELF TO
THEM, BECAUSE HE KNEW ALL PEOPLE AND NEEDED NO ONE
TO TESTIFY ABOUT ANYONE;
FOR HE HIMSELF KNEW WHAT WAS IN EVERYONE

When he had cleansed the Temple by throwing out the money changers and traders from the sacred court, Jesus had sealed his fate. It's one thing, as we all know, to teach, and another to practice. When you start to act on the truth—taking the risk about being right and the bigger risk of becoming unpopular for rocking the boat—the system will turn against you. Turkeys don't vote for Christmas and pigs don't vote for Easter.

There is, as we all know, personal sin. For example: our refusal to face reality and our preference for what we privately know to be illusion; or our deliberate, carefully self-justified hardening of heart to people in need who would benefit from our time, treasure or talent; our crafty ways of defending a self-centered relationship with the events and people in our life; our deliberate greed and short-term profit motive; our ways of exploiting people. And so on. We all know our faults—or suspect them. They are the causes of our individual, psychological hell—the domain of the false self. However painful, they present no great obstacle to the love of God welling up through our cracks to heal us and give us always another chance.

But there is something else in the realm of sin that affects us because it conditions us through the culture we live in. It is more collective and impersonal than our personal faults. We see it in social tsunamis of insanely horrific inhumanity and callousness such as the Shoah or the current violence in the Middle East. This sin possesses not just individuals but whole groups. It gives an ersatz sense of community—a perverse and self-destructive version of the solidarity that all human beings seek.

Sin, personal or collective, is sticky. Even when we try to detach ourselves from it, it becomes more attached. Victims then become like the ones that persecuted them while still presenting themselves as the underdog. How can we extricate ourselves and our world from the horrible stickiness of sin? Heavy injections of the reality serum.

The work of meditation, according to the fourteenth-century *Cloud of Unknowing*,[6] dries up the root of sin. A big claim. But true. And it won't make you popular. Meditation is a powerful dissolvent of the glue of illusion and selfishness. Like a great product we discover that does a household job we have not been able to complete, meditation does what it promises. Provided we use it. Lent is the time to get these jobs done. Keep going—it's worth it.

MONDAY
Luke 4:24–30

"And he said, 'Truly I tell you, no prophet is accepted in the prophet's home town. But the truth is, there were many widows in Israel in the time of Elijah, when the heaven was shut up for three years and six months, and there was a severe famine over all the land; yet Elijah was sent to none of them except to a widow at Zarephath in Sidon. There were also many lepers in Israel in the time of the prophet Elisha, and none of them was cleansed except Naaman the Syrian.' When they heard this, all in the synagogue were filled with rage. They got up, drove him out of the town, and led him to the brow of the hill on which their town was built, so that they might hurl him off the cliff. But he passed through the midst of them and went on his way."

TRULY I TELL YOU, NO PROPHET IS ACCEPTED IN THE PROPHET'S HOME TOWN

How could a vision of life as radically counter-cultural to the idea of worldly success ever have become a world religion, with hierarchies, strategic planners, political forces and a desire to make everyone its adherents? Because it is not frightened of sin. Because it sees its founder as 'becoming sin for our sake.' Because it's about incarnation, not sublimation.

But we should never forget—and Lent won't let us—that we cannot pursue success, acceptance, and acclaim as authentic goals of life, and be real.

Many people feel that they fail at meditation. They do. And they don't. It is true they don't achieve the perfection they are seeking and that will seem like a falling short. Many then give up because they have been conditioned by their ego to think that only success has meaning, only success is rewarded. Big error. Those who hang in there with the practice, awaken, in the process of failing, to the discovery that even though they aren't perfect, they are winning a victory they had not even imagined. It's the victory of fidelity: the force of radical transformation. In meditation we score no goals but we win the match. Most people who stay faithful to the practice find the inner freedom that comes with an embraced discipline. They will add, in a self-deprecating way, that they are not good meditators.

The experience of meditation is unlike any other. It is extremely difficult to define because it is an entry into such radical simplicity that we lose even the words to describe it. Because it gently penetrates to the deepest centre of our existence, it involves and influences everything in our life with a marvelous capacity to unify. Past and future merge into the present. Fears and obsessions melt. We see the good in our enemies. We are expanded by love and we expand the world by love. Every contemplative consciousness (this does not mean "me") is able, to some degree, to absorb evil into the good.

In the process it lowers blood pressure, reduces stress and helps us sleep better at night. These are only some of the notes of a great music of being that we become able to listen to by making meditation part of our life. We even see the music playing in daily life.

But that might put you off for sounding too mystical. With the focus of simple awareness, other-centeredness and self-knowledge that Lent develops, however, we awaken to just how simple, unified and "good"—in a way that goes deeper than any moral sense of the word—each moment of each day is. That's why we hang in and ignore the egocentric feeling of failure and don't worry what people say.

TUESDAY
Matthew 18:21–35

"Then Peter came and said to him, 'Lord, if another member of the church sins against me, how often should I forgive? As many as seven times?' Jesus said to him, 'Not seven times, but, I tell you, seventy-seven times. For this reason the kingdom of heaven may be compared to a king who wished to settle accounts with his slaves. When he began the reckoning, one who owed him ten thousand talents was brought to him; and, as he could not pay, his lord ordered him to be sold, together with his wife and children and all his possessions, and payment to be made. So the slave fell on his knees before him, saying, "Have patience with me, and I will pay you everything." And out of pity for him, the lord of that slave released him and forgave him the debt. But that same slave, as he went out, came upon one of his fellow-slaves who owed him a hundred denarii; and seizing him by the throat, he said, "Pay what you owe." Then his fellow-slave fell down and pleaded with him, "Have patience with me, and I will pay you." But he refused; then he went and threw him into prison until he should pay the debt. When his fellow-slaves saw what had happened, they were greatly distressed, and they went and reported to their lord all that had taken place. Then his lord summoned him and said to him, "You wicked slave! I forgave you all that debt because you pleaded with me. Should you not have had mercy on your fellow-slave, as I had mercy on you?" And in anger his lord handed him over to be tortured until he should pay his entire debt. So my heavenly Father will also do to every one of you, if you do not forgive your brother or sister from your heart.'"

OUT OF PITY FOR HIM, THE LORD OF THAT SLAVE RELEASED HIM AND FORGAVE HIM THE DEBT

It's called debt restructuring. And it would save a lot of time and politics if it could be practiced by the rich toward the poor in our global economy. But no verbal argument will achieve that. Such a radical revision of policy needs familiarity with the forces of silence.

A good new practice to highlight, even at this midway point in the Lenten period, is silence. Silence is the greatest of teachers. Speaking or thinking about silence can be counterproductive and even lead to arguments about different ways into silence. This is because—obviously—silence does not need to be spoken. Riddle: When you speak my name I disappear. What am I?

Yet it is necessary to think about what silence means because otherwise we may never even become conscious that silence exists. This is increasingly true in our highly distracted culture. Distraction is unnecessary noise.

I recently boarded a plane for a long flight and my heart sank as I discovered I was sitting next to two young brothers who looked very naturally boisterous. In fact, for eight hours they were both completely numbed and sedated by a combination of their iPad games and the TV screens, both of which they used continuously and simultaneously. It meant I could meditate, read, and nap during the flight, but what it suggested about the noise and overstimulation filling the minds of the young worried me greatly.

If our natural environment lacks silence, how will we ever understand what it is? We will know we have lost something, but will have no word for what it is. Silence will just mean that the audio doesn't work. So we must speak about silence, communicating what it is until the penny drops into the bottomless well. Meditation restores us to the experience of silence. It illustrates how conscious, faithful repetition leads us toward and into silence by the stilling of the mind and desire. So, I repeat, silence is the greatest of teachers.

It heals, refreshes, energizes, inspires, sharpens, clarifies. It simplifies. It is the medium of truth. And it is the font of the pure single Word that both perfectly communicates it and leads back to it. If we consciously turn off the TV or close the computer, restrain unnecessary speech, avoid gazing at advertising posters, look people lovingly in the eye, we are enhancing the same direct work of silence that we return to meeting in our meditation. And we are making the world a more silent and awakened place.

WEDNESDAY
Matthew 5:17–19

"Do not think that I have come to abolish the law or the prophets; I have come not to abolish but to fulfil. For truly I tell you, until heaven and earth pass away, not one letter, not one stroke of a letter, will pass from the law until all is accomplished. Therefore, whoever breaks one of the least of these commandments, and teaches others to do the same, will be called least in the kingdom of heaven; but whoever does them and teaches them will be called great in the kingdom of heaven."

I HAVE COME NOT TO ABOLISH BUT TO FULFIL
These recent Gospels have illustrated how Jesus dealt with criticism and rejection—the things we like least in life. His example of complete integrity inspires us to remember what wholeness means. It encourages us to think that it is humanly possible.

When we see hypocrisy—the enemy of integrity—we are cautious. If we condemn it—as Jesus and the great teachers did—we expose ourselves to attack. No one likes to be called a hypocrite, yet at some level we all know that we are. The word comes from the Greek *hypokrisis*, which means "actor." Yet it is almost inevitable that we pretend to be or feel what we are not, or do not, even if we would also like to be what we pretend. "I'm so sorry" (meaning "get over it"). "Let's change" (meaning "you first"). "I love you" (add "provided that...").

We don't have to despair about our inauthenticity, simply admit it. That defuses it and prevents our false self from blocking the way to the deeper level of consciousness on which we can only be who we are, and where the truth is not something we think or say but a completely (inter)personal experience. The sign that we are heading there is that we don't take ourselves too solemnly and that we laugh at our false self and welcome other people to do the same.

Gradually the actor's mask becomes—as in great theatre rather than in soap opera—a transparent means of revealing the deeper truth. Form can then communicate the emptiness that is fullness. (God is the union of emptiness and fullness.) The wonderful thing is that this happens—if we allow it and make the space necessary—in subtle ways and in the most ordinary things of life. (Seeing God in everyone.) That is why Lent is about small things. And why meditation is more about practice than good intention.

THURSDAY
Luke 11:14–23

"Now he was casting out a demon that was mute; when the demon had gone out, the one who had been mute spoke, and the crowds were amazed. But some of them said, 'He casts out demons by Beelzebul, the ruler of the demons.' Others, to test him, kept demanding from him a sign from heaven. But he knew what they were thinking and said to them, 'Every kingdom divided against itself becomes a desert, and house falls on house. If Satan also is divided against himself, how will his kingdom stand?—for you say that I cast out the demons by Beelzebul. Now if I cast out the demons by Beelzebul, by whom do your exorcists cast them out? Therefore they will be your judges. But if it is by the finger of God that I cast out the demons, then the kingdom of God has come to you. When a strong man, fully armed, guards his castle, his property is safe. But when one stronger than he attacks him and overpowers him, he takes away his armour in which he trusted and divides his plunder. Whoever is not with me is against me, and whoever does not gather with me scatters.'"

WHOEVER IS NOT WITH ME IS AGAINST ME; AND WHOEVER
DOES NOT GATHER WITH ME SCATTERS

I was once meditating late one evening at the beginning of a retreat. I had arrived that day after a long flight; and the flesh was weak. I knew I didn't nod off to the extent of falling off the chair, but my drowsiness made my earlier remarks about sitting upright and alert sound a little lacking in authority. The next day, one of the retreatants asked me if I used a special sitting technique during meditation. I said, "No, why do you ask?" "It's just that I was watching you," he replied, "during the meditation last night, and you were rocking to and fro. I saw some Jewish scholars reading Scripture like that once and I just wondered." My reputation was saved.

"Are you with me?" It's a question we might ask someone, or a group to whom we are talking, to make sure they haven't gone off to sleep while we were talking. Or at a critical moment in negotiations when we need to know who is on our side and who isn't. Or to a companion during a dark and dangerous walk along a cliff-edge to reassure ourselves he hasn't fallen off.

I don't think Jesus means any of these by "with me." We might still be "with him" even if we have fallen off to sleep or feel isolated in a hard place. He himself felt abandoned, but not disconnected from his Father at the end of his life—a strange and perhaps unique experience of communion and separation.

In this saying, however, I think he means a deeper knowledge than is provided by evidence-based research—what we can see or deduce. It's the knowledge that is knowing, not the knowledge stored in memory. The opposite of it is not ignorance in the usual sense of not knowing something, but "scattering." To be scattered is to have our sense of self diluted by distraction, overextended by stimulation or fragmented in myriad lines of fantasy. It is a state in which we can say or do nothing useful and in which we may be dangerous if we can pretend to be there and with it. There are people in marriages and monks in monasteries who have slipped into this state and keep up appearances but are not really there any more. Where they actually are is a mystery, especially to themselves.

This Gospel is about healing the demon of muteness, allowing the person to speak, to communicate again. Some people watching, whispered that Jesus was using demonic powers to cast out the demon, the incongruity of which he pointed out. These were the people who were not with him because they weren't anywhere that matters.

Much worse than a meditator nodding off.

FRIDAY
Mark 12:28–34

"One of the scribes came near and heard them disputing with one another, and seeing that he answered them well, he asked him, 'Which commandment is the first of all?' Jesus answered, 'The first is, "Hear, O Israel: the Lord our God, the Lord is one; you shall love the Lord your God with all your heart, and with all your soul, and with all your mind, and with all your strength." The second is this, "You shall love your neighbour as yourself." There is no other commandment greater than these.' Then the scribe said to him, 'You are right, Teacher; you have truly said that "he is one, and besides him there is no other"; and "to love him with all the heart, and with all the understanding, and with all the strength," and "to love one's neighbour as oneself,"—this is much more important than all whole burnt-offerings and sacrifices.' When Jesus saw that he answered wisely, he said to him, 'You are not far from the kingdom of God.' After that no one dared to ask him any question."

YOU SHALL LOVE THE LORD YOUR GOD WITH ALL YOUR HEART,
AND WITH ALL YOUR SOUL, AND WITH ALL YOUR MIND,
AND WITH ALL YOUR STRENGTH. THE SECOND IS THIS,
YOU SHALL LOVE YOUR NEIGHBOUR AS YOURSELF

I hope you have been memorizing these Gospel verses as I suggested, because by now you will have trained your memory, and this slightly longer one today won't be a problem. It's longer but even simpler than the rest: Jesus's answer to "Which is the most important commandment?"

Because we are so bombarded today with messages and demands, and our attention is being pulled in many different directions, we like the idea of simplicity. We may also like leaving big decisions that we should take for ourselves to other people like the government or doctors or, though less often today for obvious reasons, to clergy.

There is a plethora of courses and programs on the market offering to sort us out and give us skills we need to take control of our lives—provided we buy (and believe). Corporations and governments, distractedly aware of how much they are losing the war against distraction, are especially interested in these solutions. A spiritual solution, however, is different in a number of ways: it's been around a long time and doesn't claim to be new; it is not for financial profit; it is a discipline, not a technique; it is simple, not easy.

Today's teaching says the most important thing in life is to love God, your neighbor and yourself—equally. You will have to have become very simple before you can do this, but in the trying you will be radicalized—in the good sense—radically simplified and your capacity for love fully amplified.

Lent and meditation go nicely together (as meditation does with all the seasons) because they are both about simplicity and discovering that, when we are simple, we can do one thing and achieve infinitely more than what we may be trying to achieve.

Saturday
Luke 18:9–14

"He also told this parable to some who trusted in themselves that they were righteous and regarded others with contempt: 'Two men went up to the temple to pray, one a Pharisee and the other a tax-collector. The Pharisee, standing by himself, was praying thus, "God, I thank you that I am not like other people: thieves, rogues, adulterers, or even like this tax-collector. I fast twice a week; I give a tenth of all my income." But the tax-collector, standing far off, would not even look up to heaven, but was beating his breast and saying, "God, be merciful to me, a sinner!" I tell you, this man went down to his home justified rather than the other; for all who exalt themselves will be humbled, but all who humble themselves will be exalted.'"

FOR ALL WHO EXALT THEMSELVES WILL BE HUMBLED, BUT ALL WHO HUMBLE THEMSELVES WILL BE EXALTED

When we want to avoid details and make arguments that will sweep all opposition away, we say things like "There are two kinds of people..." or "We can do one of two things..." The mind likes dualities because there's always a winner and a loser. But, as God and the meditator know, dualities are only two-thirds of the story. The deeper, subatomic mind thinks in threes and so winning or losing isn't the main point.

As a teacher, using stories that were both simple and subtle, Jesus used the dualistic to get to the Trinitarian. In this story, two men go to the temple to pray. One is an absurd, Dickensian clerical bigot and an egoist of the first order, who really believes he's better than everyone else and thanks God for it. The other is also a stereotype, a corrupt tax collector who probably ran bars and strip clubs and other shady enterprises. What's surprising is that he was in the temple at all and was praying. Not surprisingly, the Pharisee was too self-absorbed to know that he wasn't really praying at all. He didn't know that he was distracted—by the worst of all distractions. The publican was probably trying to focus, but couldn't stop thinking of his business problems. But he knew it and threw that awareness into the pot of prayer as well. True worship swallows everything.

Like Martha and Mary, or the prodigal son and his older brother, these two seem polar opposites. But read it a second and third time and they begin to fuse. The listening mind begins to recognize itself in each of them. Don't we all have moments when we feel superior, if not to everyone else, then at least to the lowest? And don't we all have, in the murkiest corners of our ego, an awareness that we are very screwed up and can do nothing about it except open ourselves, in that very place, to the God we only discover in humility? Except we do even that imperfectly.

So what is the mind that is aware of this duality within us? The third, which makes one. Except it is a non-numerical oneness, a unity and a union in which duality is both healed and transcended in the process of meditation. And so there's the paradox by which Jesus wraps up the parable—exalt and be humbled, humble and be exalted. You obviously can't stay long in either place then. So where are we? We arrive at that non-geographical place when we see that God is smiling.

Learning to Meditate

It's good to take a few moments—or longer if you have time—to prepare for meditation and to conclude it. You could do so in this way—physical, breathing, mental.

Physically, you can stretch—stand and bend forward, stretch your arms and legs, loosen your neck and shoulders. Some like to do their regular run before meditating. The body is always in the present moment, so let it anchor you there.

Breath links body and mind—our breathing reflects the state of our mind. So, observe your breathing for a few moments. Take a few deep breaths and release them slowly. You have already started to take the attention off your thoughts.

Mentally, you may have some strong feelings to deal with, problems you are wrestling with. Acknowledge them and tell them to wait. You'll come back to them after meditation.

Then start the mantra. Let it gently, faithfully guide you to whatever level of stillness and equanimity you can reach today.

Body, breath, mind—when these are quiet the spirit blossoms.

After the meditation, wait till the last sound of the bell or timer-signal fades before opening your eyes. This is a good time to read the Gospel of the day.

Fourth Sunday of Lent
John 3:14–21

"And just as Moses lifted up the serpent in the wilderness, so must the Son of Man be lifted up, that whoever believes in him may have eternal life. For God so loved the world that he gave his only Son, so that everyone who believes in him may not perish but may have eternal life. Indeed, God did not send the Son into the world to condemn the world, but in order that the world might be saved through him. Those who believe in him are not condemned; but those who do not believe are condemned already, because they have not believed in the name of the only Son of God. And this is the judgment, that the light has come into the world, and people loved darkness rather than light because their deeds were evil. For all who do evil hate the light and do not come to the light, so that their deeds may not be exposed. But those who do what is true come to the light, so that it may be clearly seen that their deeds have been done in God."

Those who do what is true come to the light

The television news recently showed a former high-flying banker confronted by a reporter who accompanied him down the street repeating the same question about corruption and receiving the same deadpan "no comment" response. There was something very disturbing and revealing about the scene; the very public invasion of privacy and shaming exposure; the pressing demand for truth, and the refusal to speak that spoke more than words.

When the butchers of Auschwitz saw that the nightmare they had inflicted on others was now turning on them, they fled the scene of evil and tried to blow up the evidence. Today you can see the rubble they left behind, condemning them and shaming all humanity. However intense the denial, you cannot bury darkness in light.

The truth is not just what you say. You can wait for your lawyer to give you the oily words that will get you off the hook. But truth is lived, not spoken. It is what you live and how you live. Truth cannot be hidden. When the dust of the explosion that tries to destroy it settles, whatever you tried to conceal is more visible than ever.

If you have something to hide and if you are afraid of the truth, then this is the terrible, inescapable truth of truth. It will come to light, just as reality will emerge from the ashes of the illusion that tried to evade the truth. This is true not only of deeds done. It is also true of a truth repressed in our minds and memories. A feeling that is too painful to face, a mistake too hurtful to admit, an insight too transformative to welcome.

Until we come into the open and let the truth expand in the light, we will be hounded, and we will be on the run. Meditation is living the truth. In the light—in the open.

Monday
John 4:43–54

"When the two days were over, he went from that place to Galilee (for Jesus himself had testified that a prophet has no honor in the prophet's own country). When he came to Galilee, the Galileans welcomed him, since they had seen all that he had done in Jerusalem at the festival; for they too had gone to the festival. Then he came again to Cana in Galilee where he had changed the water into wine. Now there was a royal official whose son lay ill in Capernaum. When he heard that Jesus had come from Judea to Galilee, he went and begged him to come down and heal his son, for he was at the point of death. Then Jesus said to him, 'Unless you see signs and wonders you will not believe.' The official said to him, 'Sir, come down before my little boy dies.' Jesus said to him, 'Go; your son will live.' The man believed the word that Jesus spoke to him and started on his way. As he was going down, his slaves met him and told him that his child was alive. So he asked them the hour when he began to recover, and they said to him, 'Yesterday at one in the afternoon the fever left him.' The father realized that this was the hour when Jesus had said to him, 'Your son will live.' So he himself believed, along with his whole household. Now this was the second sign that Jesus did after coming from Judea to Galilee."

UNLESS YOU SEE SIGNS AND WONDERS YOU WILL NOT BELIEVE
These are the harsh-seeming words Jesus spoke to the man who came to him and asked him to come and save his dying son.

Jesus then told him his son would live, and the man went home to find that the boy had recovered at that instant. Magic or faith? This is the question that reveals the true dynamic of this story and all the Gospels.

His words to the desperate parent, quoted above, might seem to lack compassion. We might imagine ourselves being pestered to help someone in need and yet feeling we have given out enough for the day. Their intensity, however, makes us yield and give them what they want; but we haven't resolved our own feeling of self-protection, the guardedness that always prevents us from making a pure and unconditional gift of self. So we give in, but we also, unkindly, throw in a complaint or a criticism as well. OK, I'll heal your son but it's about time you stopped asking me for miracles after hours.

It doesn't feel that this is what Jesus is saying.

The father, like anyone concerned for a loved one in danger, is desperate for a miracle. Even when we have faced the truth and given up false hope, there remains a pocket of desperation where the dream of a miracle never dies. Our need for magic, for manipulating causes and effects from the outside, can even survive despair. Political crisis, economic downturns, fiction and boy wizards all evidence our appetite for the fast food of magical signs and wonders. When things are desperate, that is when we most want magical powers.

By his remark, Jesus simply exposes this and so frees the father, and us, from the addiction to magical solutions. What flows from him is the power of healing in the full force of compassion. In meditation we are saved from our own desperation, not by the external signs of magic, but by what is already within us, where we are already in touch with the power we project and seek outside ourselves.

Jesus didn't want people to see him as a magician or even as a messiah. He wanted more, for people to connect with him, to know him, from within themselves. There are also signs and wonders associated with that. But they are not magical. They are the real signs of a wondrous transformation of self, produced by the relationship we call faith.

TUESDAY
John 5:1–16

"After this there was a festival of the Jews, and Jesus went up to Jerusalem. Now in Jerusalem by the Sheep Gate there is a pool, called in Hebrew Bethzatha, which has five porticoes. In these lay many invalids—blind, lame, and paralysed. One man was there who had been ill for thirty-eight years. When Jesus saw him lying there and knew that he had been there a long time, he said to him, 'Do you want to be made well?' The sick man answered him, 'Sir, I have no one to put me into the pool when the water is stirred up; and while I am making my way, someone else steps down ahead of me.' Jesus said to him, 'Stand up, take your mat and walk.' At once the man was made well, and he took up his mat and began to walk. Now that day was a sabbath. So the Jews said to the man who had been cured, 'It is the sabbath; it is not lawful for you to carry your mat.' But he answered them, 'The man who made me well said to me, "Take up your mat and walk."' They asked him, 'Who is the man who said to you, "Take it up and walk"?' Now the man who had been healed did not know who it was, for Jesus had disappeared in the crowd that was there. Later Jesus found him in the temple and said to him, 'See, you have been made well! Do not sin any more, so that nothing worse happens to you.' The man went away and told the Jews that it was Jesus who had made him well. Therefore the Jews started persecuting Jesus, because he was doing such things on the sabbath."

STAND UP, TAKE YOUR MAT AND WALK

The man healed in this story complains that no one has helped him to get into the magic pool while the angel was stirring the waters. He has been waiting there for thirty-eight barren years: as long, according to Deuteronomy, as the Israelites had wandered in the desert.

What's the symbolism of that? Are there problems, blocks, hang-ups in yourself, in your character, in your life, that have been with you for as long as you remember? Things that you have given up on ever getting over but which still cause you to regret, complain or feel sorry for yourself? The cause of the problem, however much it is ancient history, set deep in the early layers of your life, is linked to and sustained by the effects of the sadness or anger it has produced.

So we are held in a double pincer movement: a historical trauma and an ongoing post-traumatic stress. The past has flooded and incapacitated the present, just as a computer virus invades and slows down operational functions. We are held captive and we feel no one seems to want, or to be able to help.

The spirit cannot tolerate such a situation and such a waste. Given half a chance, even a brief encounter by a magical pool, it will penetrate the person and target the problem and say, "Now move on and take that damned mat with you." This is what is happening in meditation.

Wednesday
John 5:17–30

"But Jesus answered them, 'My Father is still working, and I also am working.' For this reason the Jews were seeking all the more to kill him, because he was not only breaking the sabbath, but was also calling God his own Father, thereby making himself equal to God. Jesus said to them, 'Very truly, I tell you, the Son can do nothing on his own, but only what he sees the Father doing; for whatever the Father does, the Son does likewise. The Father loves the Son and shows him all that he himself is doing; and he will show him greater works than these, so that you will be astonished. Indeed, just as the Father raises the dead and gives them life, so also the Son gives life to whomsoever he wishes. The Father judges no one but has given all judgment to the Son, so that all may honor the Son just as they honor the Father. Anyone who does not honor the Son does not honor the Father who sent him. Very truly, I tell you, anyone who hears my word and believes in him who sent me has eternal life, and does not come under judgment, but has passed from death to life. Very truly, I tell you, the hour is coming, and is now here, when the dead will hear the voice of the Son of God, and those who hear will live. For just as the Father has life in himself, so he has granted the Son also to have life in himself; and he has given him authority to execute judgment, because he is the Son of Man. Do not be astonished at this; for the hour is coming when all who are in their graves will hear his voice and will come out—those who have done good, to the resurrection of life, and those who have done evil, to the resurrection of condemnation. I can do nothing on my own. As I hear, I judge; and my judgment is just, because I seek to do not my own will but the will of him who sent me.'"

I SEEK TO DO NOT MY OWN WILL
BUT THE WILL OF HIM WHO SENT ME

Friends are people who are there for us when we need them. Often we don't know who among our acquaintances are true friends until circumstances reveal it. People we thought we could rely on conveniently aren't available or sit on the fence when we need people on our side. Others, whom we had not really appreciated before, show an unexpected depth of love and courage.

This being-there-for of friendship applies not only in times when external events overwhelm us and we feel helpless and alone. Friends also, on occasion, save us from ourselves. Our inner high and low pressures threaten us with a personal implosion. A friend knows us well enough to recognize this and does not walk away even when we push him away. He waits and does not take offence. (Love is patient and kind.) If we do not reach out to a friend suffering in this type of isolation, even when he rejects our offer of help, we fail ourselves, our friend and the friendship itself.

Friendship, like the relationship that Jesus describes himself having with his "Father," is like the digital cloud. Everything here down below is stored up there, non-geographically, but accessible from any physical point and at every moment. Both friends are there together in the cloud. But they are also individuals, living the friendship in all the changing circumstances of life.

Perhaps this helps us understand why the way this relationship with the Father is described sounds both deeply intimate and way beyond our grasp. In certain dimensions of consciousness we find ourselves at what physics calls an "event horizon." As observers, we feel it is all obscure and distant; we feel we are traveling to a point of no return. But if we stop trying to observe we suddenly feel at home, and at peace as never before.

We need to train for this awakening. The point of Lent is training in order to remain more aware and alert in ordinary life so that we experience how extraordinary it is.

THURSDAY
Luke 2:41–51

"Now every year his parents went to Jerusalem for the festival of the Passover. And when he was twelve years old, they went up as usual for the festival. When the festival was ended and they started to return, the boy Jesus stayed behind in Jerusalem, but his parents did not know it. Assuming that he was in the group of travellers, they went a day's journey. Then they started to look for him among their relatives and friends. When they did not find him, they returned to Jerusalem to search for him. After three days they found him in the temple, sitting among the teachers, listening to them and asking them questions. And all who heard him were amazed at his understanding and his answers. When his parents saw him they were astonished; and his mother said to him, 'Child, why have you treated us like this? Look, your father and I have been searching for you in great anxiety.' He said to them, 'Why were you searching for me? Did you not know that I must be in my Father's house?' But they did not understand what he said to them. Then he went down with them and came to Nazareth, and was obedient to them. His mother treasured all these things in her heart."

"WHY WERE YOU SEARCHING FOR ME?
DID YOU NOT KNOW THAT I MUST BE IN MY FATHER'S HOUSE?"
BUT THEY DID NOT UNDERSTAND WHAT HE SAID TO THEM

One afternoon, I went bike riding with my young godson. He was reluctant to end the trip and zoomed off ahead of me around a bend in the path. When I turned the corner, he had disappeared. There followed one of the worst half hours of my life. Every ambulance or police siren filled me with horror and I saw the worst in everyone passing by. I tried to control my fears but they kept flooding in. Eventually he turned up, smiling broadly and asking me where I had been and why I had kept him waiting. My relief was so great I could only pretend to be angry.

It's a very human story about our concern for the young in our care and one that St. Luke tells in this Gospel. Mary and Joseph both thought for a whole day that the twelve-year-old Jesus was in the other's company. They rushed back to look for him and found him in the temple discussing God with the teachers there. They rebuked him for the anxiety he had caused and he answered with these slightly extraterrestrial-sounding words that they did not understand. It's an example of how a real incident becomes theologized in the remembering and retelling, and is made to convey more than you would first think it could. We all do this too, as we make neatly cut stories out of the randomness of our lives.

We slice up experience into beginnings, middles and ends and draw lessons from the slices. We stock our mental shelves with these stories, often adding to or refreshing them according to what we sense our listeners would like. The Irish make a living from this. Reality at the cutting edge, however, is characterized by frayed ends and incomplete conclusions. *Chaos* is another word for it, one that we don't like to use about our lives. But we walk a very thin line between cosmos (order) and chaos, and most of the order we put into things has a tendency to unravel very quickly.

Even when we get the key to understanding its meaning, like Jesus's poor parents, we don't understand it. But he went back and lived with them anyway which, for the time, was evidently enough. In the self-discipline of Lenten meditation, which sharpens our daily awareness, we get deeper and more piercing glimpses into this provisionality of life and, strangely, we even find it reassuring.

FRIDAY
John 7:1–2, 10, 25–30

"After this Jesus went about in Galilee. He did not wish to go about in Judea because the Jews were looking for an opportunity to kill him. Now the Jewish festival of Booths was near... But after his brothers had gone to the festival, then he also went, not publicly but as it were in secret... Now some of the people of Jerusalem were saying, 'Is not this the man whom they are trying to kill? And here he is, speaking openly, but they say nothing to him! Can it be that the authorities really know that this is the Messiah? Yet we know where this man is from; but when the Messiah comes, no one will know where he is from.' Then Jesus cried out as he was teaching in the temple, 'You know me, and you know where I am from. I have not come on my own. But the one who sent me is true, and you do not know him. I know him, because I am from him, and he sent me.' Then they tried to arrest him, but no one laid hands on him, because his hour had not yet come."

JESUS WENT ABOUT IN GALILEE

He walked and talked and, of course, walked the talk. He wasn't publishing or doing interviews or checking with his PR advisors or even writing reflections. We don't know if he had a schedule or made appointments. The sense is that he was present wherever he was and saw the depth dimension, the eternal, lucidly present in everyone and every occasion. He was spontaneous but not a drifter. He met reality continually, and reality was always rushing to meet him. Because of the tang of reality they emit, such people are powerfully attractive, although often frightening too, when we get close.

Francis of Assisi seems to have been such a person. Ramana Maharshi, who never moved from the place in which he settled at the age of sixteen, was, odd though it may sound, another. He was asked once why he didn't travel the world, bringing his peace to the masses where it was needed. "How do you know I don't?" he replied.

When Yeshua moved about Galilee he was a consistently steady, still point manifesting in many places. People who stay at home but fantasize about trips and being elsewhere do not have anything like this stability. St. Benedict says the monk "must prefer nothing to Christ." Quite soon in my monastic life I heard the ironical version of this, "prefer nothing to a trip," from monks who had come to understand stability primarily in geographical terms.

Of course we can also be on the move as a way of keeping one step ahead of reality, being on the run from something and protecting ourselves from it. But stability, whether you are busy or not, is a fruit of meditation. The morning and evening sessions emit a pulse that keeps everything aligned. It produces the clarity, discernment and good judgment that improves the quality and other-centeredness of our lives. Stability brings the point of departure and the place of arrival together in a dynamic stillness and a radical openness to change. Not a bad goal to identify, even in the last part of Lent.

SATURDAY
John 7:40–52

"When they heard these words, some in the crowd said, 'This is really the prophet.' Others said, 'This is the Messiah.' But some asked, 'Surely the Messiah does not come from Galilee, does he? Has not the scripture said that the Messiah is descended from David and comes from Bethlehem, the village where David lived?' So there was a division in the crowd because of him. Some of them wanted to arrest him, but no one laid hands on him. Then the temple police went back to the chief priests and Pharisees, who asked them, 'Why did you not arrest him?' The police answered, 'Never has anyone spoken like this!' Then the Pharisees replied, 'Surely you have not been deceived too, have you? Has any one of the authorities or of the Pharisees believed in him? But this crowd, which does not know the law—they are accursed.' Nicodemus, who had gone to Jesus before, and who was one of them, asked, 'Our law does not judge people without first giving them a hearing to find out what they are doing, does it?' They replied, 'Surely you are not also from Galilee, are you? Search and you will see that no prophet is to arise from Galilee.'"

SO THERE WAS A DIVISION IN THE CROWD BECAUSE OF HIM
You have only to be truthful to cause trouble. But it's a different kind of trouble when you are untruthful. You have to decide what kind of troublemaker you will be. Perhaps most people want to avoid causing any trouble because they are frightened

of a backlash; but eventually we all have to decide. Are we going to tell the truth, to live the truth or to hide behind platitudes and half-truths?

Trouble means conflict and conflict means division. Division frequently means violence. A heightened level of awareness can prevent this sequence from unfolding and allow us to make the right decision to be truthful even when this carries a high cost. The truth will set you free. When meditators experience this incremental liberation from fear and evasion, they more readily come out into the open to say what they really mean. And they stand on the side of those in need rather than merely on the side of those who will be the likely winners in a conflict.

At first this is uncomfortable, like going out into the winter cold from a warm house. You may be well wrapped up but the cold still seems to creep in through the gaps or to attack your teeth as you walk along puffing with your mouth open. But then, after a while, your walking in the cold air produces warmth and the cold itself becomes a stimulant. You are making friends with the winter and you are surprised by your own resilience.

In the mysterious paradoxes of reality it can often happen that divisions are necessary to create healing and a stronger union. We break the bread in order to share it and be brought into unity. The mystery here is that of separation, which is necessary for us to know ourselves before we can give ourselves to another, to God. We know this because we are like God, and God knows it, as the coming days will remind us.

Still Learning to Meditate

Time for some self-evaluation; how regularly are you meditating? Have you developed a routine—time, place, way of preparation, and conclusion? How often do you do the full twenty minutes?

Are you doing the best you can? If so, you get 100 percent.

Your meditation in the morning sends you out into the day with a fresh experience of peace and joy, deeper than your thoughts, feelings, and problems. Like the smell of fresh bread and newly brewed coffee.

Your evening meditation closes the work of the day with acceptance and humility. You offer it to God—imperfect as it is—and let it go. No wonder you may sleep better as a result.

But the day in between is a kind of prayer too; your work and your response to events. Take the opportunities for brief times of prayerful presence—waiting for and in the elevator, in between appointments, before eating or having coffee, sitting in a traffic jam or even just at the lights.

Let the mantra rise in your heart at these moments and you will begin to feel what "continuous" prayer means.

Meditation prepares you for the day. The day prepares you for meditation.

Fifth Sunday of Lent
John 12:20–33

"Now among those who went up to worship at the festival were some Greeks. They came to Philip, who was from Bethsaida in Galilee, and said to him, 'Sir, we wish to see Jesus.' Philip went and told Andrew; then Andrew and Philip went and told Jesus. Jesus answered them, 'The hour has come for the Son of Man to be glorified. Very truly, I tell you, unless a grain of wheat falls into the earth and dies, it remains just a single grain; but if it dies, it bears much fruit. Those who love their life lose it, and those who hate their life in this world will keep it for eternal life. Whoever serves me must follow me, and where I am, there will my servant be also. Whoever serves me, the Father will honor. Now my soul is troubled. And what should I say—"Father, save me from this hour"? No, it is for this reason that I have come to this hour. Father, glorify your name.' Then a voice came from heaven, 'I have glorified it, and I will glorify it again.' The crowd standing there heard it and said that it was thunder. Others said, 'An angel has spoken to him.' Jesus answered, 'This voice has come for your sake, not for mine. Now is the judgment of this world; now the ruler of this world will be driven out. And I, when I am lifted up from the earth, will draw all people to myself.' He said this to indicate the kind of death he was to die."

IT IS FOR THIS REASON THAT I HAVE COME TO THIS HOUR
The human mind can be very reactive. We don't get what we want and we rage, complain, or attack whatever we can blame

for the disappointment. It is astonishing how cruel and irrational we can be even over relatively minor things, when things don't go our way. At such times we dig our heels more deeply into the mud of negativity and anger, even though, in doing so, we increase our own pain and the distance between us and others.

Pain and sadness usually separate and isolate us. Sometimes they even sever us from the very hand that stretches out offering to save us by connecting us again to a source of compassion and healing. To another. Pain and anger can make a violent combustion, which we darkly enjoy even as it harms us.

Reacting—or responding? The trained mind with access to the spiritual intelligence of the heart, the knowledge we call wisdom, responds rather than reacts. Even in the midst of loss and confusion and fear, we can learn to choose another way. Rather than the reaction of anger there is the response of acceptance. Simply accepting what is. In that openness to truth—the truth is what is—to which meditation guides us, the option for violence dissolves. We see with a higher reason that violence is a terrible lack of imagination.

This is why I am here, facing all this, Jesus said. When we respond to events in this way we leave the past behind and a bright light from behind us illuminates the road ahead.

MONDAY
John 8:1–11

"Jesus went to the Mount of Olives. Early in the morning he came again to the temple. All the people came to him and he sat down and began to teach them. The scribes and the Pharisees brought a woman who had been caught in adultery; and making her stand before all of them, they said to him, 'Teacher, this woman was caught in the very act of committing adultery. Now in the law Moses commanded us to stone such women. Now what do you say?' They said this to test him, so that they might have some charge to bring against him. Jesus bent down and wrote with his finger on the ground. When they kept on questioning him, he straightened up and said to them, 'Let anyone among you who is without sin be the first to throw a stone at her.' And once again he bent down and wrote on the ground. When they heard it, they went away, one by one, beginning with the elders; and Jesus was left alone with the woman standing before him. Jesus straightened up and said to her, 'Woman, where are they? Has no one condemned you?' She said, 'No one, sir.' And Jesus said, 'Neither do I condemn you. Go your way, and from now on do not sin again.'"

LET ANYONE AMONG YOU WHO IS WITHOUT SIN
BE THE FIRST TO THROW A STONE AT HER

The wisdom of Solomon is so obvious and irrefutable once someone has had the clarity and courage to express it.

Clarity grows with the spirit of acceptance and the purifying of the mind. We can't conceptualize this clarity, any more than we can look at a perfectly translucent screen. We see through it. The 'vision of God' is simple seeing, not looking at. With this vision that is the result of a pure heart, we can see with clarity through all the illusions and self-deceptions, all the games the ego plays.

But this clarity separates the one who sees with it from the crowd, one like the crowd that ganged up on the woman caught in adultery. Don't we like to feel that we are right and better and then to feel our little ego magnified by the self-righteous people around us? It's the effect of a chanting crowd in a football stadium or a racist attack, or a gang rape. We reinforce and flatter each other by targeting someone weaker who may be innocent or who has been caught doing something wrong. Our anger at the victim hides our own shame.

It takes the courage of such clarity to break with the crowd and stand for the truth. Even in this story, though, Jesus doesn't touch the hearts of the crowd who were about to stone the woman. He simply removes from them the false reasoning and justification for their actions. Temporarily their collective ego was pricked and so their individual little egos deflated. But how they must have hated him when they got home and talked about it. We hope that, by then, the woman had got safely away. Jesus, however, was their new target.

Being clear and being compassionate doesn't equate with social success.

TUESDAY
John 8:21–30

"Again he said to them, 'I am going away, and you will search for me, but you will die in your sin. Where I am going, you cannot come.' Then the Jews said, 'Is he going to kill himself? Is that what he means by saying, "Where I am going, you cannot come"?' He said to them, 'You are from below, I am from above; you are of this world, I am not of this world. I told you that you would die in your sins, for you will die in your sins unless you believe that I am he.' They said to him, 'Who are you?' Jesus said to them, 'Why do I speak to you at all? I have much to say about you and much to condemn; but the one who sent me is true, and I declare to the world what I have heard from him.' They did not understand that he was speaking to them about the Father. So Jesus said, 'When you have lifted up the Son of Man, then you will realize that I am he, and that I do nothing on my own, but I speak these things as the Father instructed me. And the one who sent me is with me; he has not left me alone, for I always do what is pleasing to him.' As he was saying these things, many believed in him."

I AM NOT OF THIS WORLD

Perhaps we never truly feel we belong to this world, even if we cling to it, make it serve us, and try to get it to accept us.

Some years ago, I met a politician in transition. She (let's say) had sat high up in the realms of power and pulled and controlled many levers. He (let's say) had by no means lost all his idealism in the process, but he was finely tuned to the realities of politics as the art of the possible. He was a survivor, and the more he survived, the more ambitious he became. Survival was equivalent to success and, even if the successes were short-lived, they built up into an addiction. Then her term finished and she was in the no-man's-land of politics in which no career lasts long, without profile, responsibility, or contact with the burning issues of the day.

This politician had pause for thought even as the experience of being "out of power" generated new hopes and strategies about how to reenter the stadium. This pause is similar to the opportunity MBA students have in the break in their careers when they study to make themselves more valuable commodities, but also to reflect on the meaning of their life and work.

This necessary detachment from the market forces of power and egotism can, however, be cultivated even while engaging with those forces. We call this cultivation of detachment, which allows us to see and relate to the world as it is, "regular meditation." Learning how to meditate regularly is what we call the asceticism, spiritual practice or discipline.

Lent is first about remembering that we need such a discipline in our lives, because the world as we see it doesn't exist any more than do permanent success or immortality. We relate to the real world as soon as we can say, "I do not belong to this world." Only then may we have something useful to give to the world and be able to serve others in the games of thrones.

WEDNESDAY
John 8:31–42

"Then Jesus said to the Jews who had believed in him, 'If you continue in my word, you are truly my disciples; and you will know the truth, and the truth will make you free.' They answered him, 'We are descendants of Abraham and have never been slaves to anyone. What do you mean by saying, "You will be made free"?' Jesus answered them, 'Very truly, I tell you, everyone who commits sin is a slave to sin. The slave does not have a permanent place in the household; the son has a place there for ever. So if the Son makes you free, you will be free indeed. I know that you are descendants of Abraham; yet you look for an opportunity to kill me, because there is no place in you for my word. I declare what I have seen in the Father's presence; as for you, you should do what you have heard from the Father.' They answered him, 'Abraham is our father.' Jesus said to them, 'If you were Abraham's children, you would be doing what Abraham did, but now you are trying to kill me, a man who has told you the truth that I heard from God. This is not what Abraham did. You are indeed doing what your father does.' They said to him, 'We are not illegitimate children; we have one father, God himself.' Jesus said to them, 'If God were your Father, you would love me, for I came from God and now I am here. I did not come on my own, but he sent me.'"

IF YOU CONTINUE IN MY WORD,
YOU ARE TRULY MY DISCIPLES;
AND YOU WILL KNOW THE TRUTH,
AND THE TRUTH WILL MAKE YOU FREE

Another illustration of the fact that Jesus was not an easy person to be with, and still isn't. His insight here is sharply deeper than those to whom he is speaking. He sees into their reasons for blocking his truth and protecting themselves from its influence. He sees too, better than they at this point, that they would be prepared to kill him to protect themselves from his subversive and destabilizing vision of reality.

He claims that the source of this vision is his relationship with the truth—the "Father"—that which has given him a new human birth and way of being. This is painfully direct because we must either reject it as bombastic egotism or accept it, take down all our defenses, and reconstruct a new life and society from the ruins of our own self-importance. He is not peddling some doctrinal orthodoxy though, but simply saying "I have my origin in God." You can make an appointment and discuss with him personally what "God" means.

But what is he saying that is so true? That truth is relational, and that truth sets us free. The challenge here is that the relationship involved is so painfully personal, absolute, and uncompromising. It is total openness and transparency. Who among us can live with that for very long? Even the best relationships, lasting decades, can include secrets and no-go areas.

He further provokes us because his sense of truth and freedom gives a wholly new meaning to what freedom really means; not the ability to do what we want, fulfill our desires, and adjust our values to circumstances, always fudging the boundaries between self and reality, but freedom from any form of compulsion (what he calls being enslaved) and from any trace of fear. He is either insane or fearless, free as the sky or entirely manipulated by his ego. As I say, he is not an easy person to know.

THURSDAY
John 8:51–59

"'Very truly, I tell you, whoever keeps my word will never see death.' The Jews said to him, 'Now we know that you have a demon. Abraham died, and so did the prophets; yet you say, "Whoever keeps my word will never taste death." Are you greater than our father Abraham, who died? The prophets also died. Who do you claim to be?' Jesus answered, 'If I glorify myself, my glory is nothing. It is my Father who glorifies me, he of whom you say, "He is our God," though you do not know him. But I know him; if I were to say that I do not know him, I would be a liar like you. But I do know him and I keep his word. Your ancestor Abraham rejoiced that he would see my day; he saw it and was glad.' Then the Jews said to him, 'You are not yet fifty years old, and have you seen Abraham?' Jesus said to them, 'Very truly, I tell you, before Abraham was, I am.' So they picked up stones to throw at him, but Jesus hid himself and went out of the temple."

BEFORE ABRAHAM WAS, I AM

The world's most powerful digital camera is being constructed in the Andes to photograph the invisible—galaxies up to eight billion light years away. It is part of a project to discover the "dark universe" of energy that science cannot understand. The existing standard model explaining the cosmos is generally accepted now to be incomplete and unsatisfying.

The exploration of dark matter involves the search for new

"super-particles," which, it is imagined, can pass through ordinary matter without any perceived interaction. This means that even the deepest parts of intergalactic space may be found to exist in an all-pervasive energy field different from anything known so far. Scientists are exploring the possibility of multiple universes, each of which has a different law of physics. At the Big Bang, which brought time and space into existence, equal amounts of matter and anti-matter also came into existence. These same scientists are wondering where the other half of the universe is hiding.

The most rational and scientific minds in the world, which are engaged in this research, are thrilled by sailing on the edge of these new continents of knowledge. The way of unknowing is always the way to deeper gnosis, fuller knowing. "To know it, though it is beyond knowledge," as St. Paul writes in his letter to the Ephesians (3:19, NEB), about the mystery of God revealed in Christ.

We need all the updated metaphors we can get to help us move toward this receding horizon that we cross in silence. The silence of the great I AM. Then we discover, no doubt, that what is eight billion light years away and which we can only know as the past is, no less, here and now.

What an exciting reason to be making our own exploration of the truth in our daily meditation. How interesting to think of the Scriptures as the coded map on this journey.

FRIDAY
John 10:31–42

"The Jews took up stones again to stone him. Jesus replied, 'I have shown you many good works from the Father. For which of these are you going to stone me?' The Jews answered, 'It is not for a good work that we are going to stone you, but for blasphemy, because you, though only a human being, are making yourself God.' Jesus answered, 'Is it not written in your law, "I said, you are gods"? If those to whom the word of God came were called "gods"—and the scripture cannot be annulled—can you say that the one whom the Father has sanctified and sent into the world is blaspheming because I said, "I am God's Son"? If I am not doing the works of my Father, then do not believe me. But if I do them, even though you do not believe me, believe the works, so that you may know and understand that the Father is in me and I am in the Father.' Then they tried to arrest him again, but he escaped from their hands. He went away again across the Jordan to the place where John had been baptizing earlier, and he remained there. Many came to him, and they were saying, 'John performed no sign, but everything that John said about this man was true.' And many believed in him there."

THE FATHER IS IN ME AND I AM IN THE FATHER
Any way of life or activity that trains us to take the attention off ourselves is worthy to be called spiritual. On the other hand, there are many things called "spiritual" which, practiced in the wrong way, can make us increasingly self-centered.

Raising a family may be exhausting and seem to leave little time for specific "spiritual practice," but it is all about other-centeredness. It is a good preparation for meditation. Conversely, monastic life may give us time for prayer but may also keep us in a shallow state of dissatisfaction, repeating the same unproductive cycles of thought and behavior. But it can be a good preparation for serving the world.

We are attracted to the other-centered option because we crave relationship and connection, which, combined, deliver us into the experience of meaning. Marriage, family, friendship, community, service are all ways in which we can learn to pay attention to others. Very quickly, however, we realize that other-centeredness is hard to do and even harder to sustain. Yet we also realize that we are better, more free and more open to love when we are learning to live in this way. Then we see that the spiritual path is a work. In fact, it is a work of love.

We no longer assume that monks must be better meditators than married people. We understand that the spiritual value of any lifestyle is measured by how it gives us opportunities for turning away from self, allowing us to find our self in the other, free from the constant self-mirroring of the ego.

The Gospels show a Jesus who was neither married nor a monk. Where did he learn that God was in him and he in God? And how did he learn how to communicate this experience of the 'kingdom' to ordinary people in such simple and profound teachings? What led him ultimately to the complete other-centeredness in which he laid down his life?

We know he went into his Lent of forty days and emerged having mastered his ego drives and powered with the Spirit to fulfill his mission. We know that he withdrew regularly to places and times of silence and stillness. Perhaps that is all we need to know—that he knew himself—in order to see that he is our teacher. And later, perhaps, to discover how he is also our way to the Father.

SATURDAY
John 11:45–56

"Many of the Jews therefore, who had come with Mary and had seen what Jesus did, believed in him. But some of them went to the Pharisees and told them what he had done. So the chief priests and the Pharisees called a meeting of the council, and said, 'What are we to do? This man is performing many signs. If we let him go on like this, everyone will believe in him, and the Romans will come and destroy both our holy place and our nation.' But one of them, Caiaphas, who was high priest that year, said to them, 'You know nothing at all! You do not understand that it is better for you to have one man die for the people than to have the whole nation destroyed.' He did not say this on his own, but being high priest that year he prophesied that Jesus was about to die for the nation, and not for the nation only, but to gather into one the dispersed children of God. So from that day on they planned to put him to death. Jesus therefore no longer walked about openly among the Jews, but went from there to a town called Ephraim in the region near the wilderness; and he remained there with the disciples. Now the Passover of the Jews was near, and many went up from the country to Jerusalem before the Passover to purify themselves. They were looking for Jesus and were asking one another as they stood in the temple, 'What do you think? Surely he will not come to the festival, will he?'"

JESUS…WENT FROM THERE TO A TOWN…
IN THE REGION NEAR THE WILDERNESS,
AND HE REMAINED THERE WITH THE DISCIPLES

In the pre-take-off instructions on a plane you are usually told that, in the case of an emergency, you should leave everything behind, even your shoes. I wonder how many would try to take their handbag or laptop or get their documents out of a bag in the overhead compartment. It must be as difficult in such a crisis as it is in daily meditation to leave everything behind. But that's things and thoughts.

When the 9/11 passengers were preparing for their end it seems they had one concern. They must have been terrifyingly pushed into complete detachment, as a condemned person waiting execution or someone with a terminal illness. Many of them wanted only to phone the people they loved and tell them they loved them.

At critical moments in his life, Jesus was in solitude, but was solitary with his close disciples. When he knew he was a marked man waiting for the midnight knock on the door, or in his case the betrayer's kiss in the garden, his instinct was to go near to the desert—a place associated both with solitude and with the deepest of all relationships, in the ground of being. And he went there with those human beings whom he understood best and who, for all their failings, understood him best.

Solitude is truthful and often delightful, even when painful. Loneliness is a hell made up of the illusion of separateness. In solitude we are capable of strong and deep relationship because in solitude we discover our uniqueness, even (or perhaps, especially) if that uniqueness is associated with death.

If meditation is about getting free from attachments and going to the desert of solitude, it is also about the discovery of the communion with others we call community. Knowing that we are with fellow disciples in the presence of our teacher is, even when things are falling apart, a source of incomparable joy.

Always Learning to Meditate

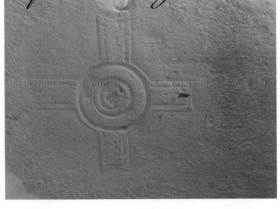

If you have begun to develop a regular practice over the past few weeks, you have doubtless discovered a new kind of experience. Have you a sense of what this experience means? Is it a new kind of awareness, of stillness in motion, of silence in words and noise, of simplicity in complex and stressful situations? Have you felt how it has influenced your four kinds of relationship—with yourself, with others, with the world, with Christ in God?

Blending this experience of contemplation with the other kinds of experience in daily life is challenging. Even though you feel the benefits of meditation, the day-to-day anxieties get in the way and may even prevent you from actually sitting. That's all right provided you don't lose touch with—or lose faith in—the simplicity of meditation.

Go back to basics as often as you can and remind yourself of how simple and immediate meditation is: sit still, close your eyes, say your mantra, let go of thoughts. Twenty minutes. Morning and evening.

Have you grasped the meaning of this simplicity yet—and how the daily meditation makes every week holy?

PALM SUNDAY
Mark 14:1–15

"It was two days before the Passover and the festival of Unleavened Bread. The chief priests and the scribes were looking for a way to arrest Jesus by stealth and kill him; for they said, 'Not during the festival, or there may be a riot among the people.' While he was at Bethany in the house of Simon the leper, as he sat at the table, a woman came with an alabaster jar of very costly ointment of nard, and she broke open the jar and poured the ointment on his head. But some were there who said to one another in anger, 'Why was the ointment wasted in this way? For this ointment could have been sold for more than three hundred denarii, and the money given to the poor.' And they scolded her. But Jesus said, 'Let her alone; why do you trouble her? She has performed a good service for me. For you always have the poor with you, and you can show kindness to them whenever you wish; but you will not always have me. She has done what she could; she has anointed my body beforehand for its burial. Truly I tell you, wherever the good news is proclaimed in the whole world, what she has done will be told in remembrance of her.' Then Judas Iscariot, who was one of the twelve, went to the chief priests in order to betray him to them. When they heard it, they were greatly pleased, and promised to give him money. So he began to look for an opportunity to betray him. On the first day of Unleavened Bread, when the Passover lamb is sacrificed, his disciples said to him, 'Where do you want us to go and make the preparations for you to eat the Passover?'

So he sent two of his disciples, saying to them, 'Go into the city, and a man carrying a jar of water will meet you; follow him, and wherever he enters, say to the owner of the house, "The Teacher asks, Where is my guest room where I may eat the Passover with my disciples?" He will show you a large room upstairs, furnished and ready. Make preparations for us there.'"

SHE BROKE OPEN THE JAR
AND POURED THE OINTMENT ON HIS HEAD

Those who care for the dying say that the most important ingredient in a good death is meaning. And meaning means connection. The sense of belonging, of being linked to another or to otherness itself.

Meaning is more than explanation. Explanations, dogma, ring hollow at such times of unavoidable encounter with reality. (How we do anything to avoid reality!) At these times we find ourselves totally defenseless and exposed in front of the tribunal of reality. Concept turns into truth and we'd like to run as far away from it as possible.

It is the totality of it that matters, and this makes the Passion of the Christ so absolute and so much of a portal for all humanity to enter utter, undifferentiated, stark reality. Then we are led into a form of experience so outside our realm of comfort and familiarity that we can neither explain nor control it.

It just happens—a devastating loss or disappointment, a reversal of expectations or dreams, a turning upside down of, well, everything. At such times our only defense is our sense of defenselessness. Because it is the only thing there is, it is the most authentic thing we can identify with. Not just our weakness, but our acceptance of our weakness, proves—against all the odds—to be our strength and resilience. This transports us from the universe of the ego—which is a reflection and false representation of reality—into another world.

But how can we take refuge in helplessness?

A sign manifests. A woman of questionable reputation breaks a jar and wastes a precious ointment and pours it on our head. In the other world, it could have been sold and the money used to promote sustainable development of an organization. But in this world, it becomes a symbol. It tells us that breaking can be healing. That sacrifice can mean homage. That what seems a futile gesture may change the entire perception of anyone with eyes to see.

Today, we start entering into what the past forty days in the desert have been preparing us for.

At first, meditation makes us more painfully aware of all the ways the ego hijacks our reactions and controls our decisions. Then it shows us that we can change our imprisoning patterns and rewire the whole ego system. Now we begin to see how this works.

When did you last have someone pour precious ointment on your head? As Rumi, the thirteenth-century Sufi poet, said: "You are a sign, and a seeker after a sign; there is no better sign than the seeker after a sign."[7]

MONDAY OF HOLY WEEK
John 12:1–11

"Six days before the Passover Jesus came to Bethany, the home of Lazarus, whom he had raised from the dead. There they gave a dinner for him. Martha served, and Lazarus was one of those at the table with him. Mary took a pound of costly perfume made of pure nard, anointed Jesus' feet, and wiped them with her hair. The house was filled with the fragrance of the perfume. But Judas Iscariot, one of his disciples (the one who was about to betray him), said, 'Why was this perfume not sold for three hundred denarii and the money given to the poor?' (He said this not because he cared about the poor, but because he was a thief; he kept the common purse and used to steal what was put into it.) Jesus said, 'Leave her alone. She bought it so that she might keep it for the day of my burial. You always have the poor with you, but you do not always have me.' When the great crowd of the Jews learned that he was there, they came not only because of Jesus but also to see Lazarus, whom he had raised from the dead. So the chief priests planned to put Lazarus to death as well, since it was on account of him that many of the Jews were deserting and were believing in Jesus."

YOU ALWAYS HAVE THE POOR WITH YOU, BUT YOU DO NOT ALWAYS HAVE ME

This is how Jesus pushes in our face the meaning of the wasting of the precious ointment. It's rather embarrassing. What greater value could there be in his system of values than caring for the poor? How can he place himself and this futile symbolic gesture above that value?

Isn't he opening the door to all the abuses of his teaching down through history that claimed to be done in his name: the torturing of heretics, the Crusades, the power games of the Church, the raising of human laws above the law of God, excommunication pronounced with a smile? And (perhaps even worse) the dilution of the gospel into a tea ceremony, the domestication of sacrament into civil ceremony, the use of community to preserve the class system, Christianity reduced to flower-arrangement?

His surprising words indicate that we are embarking, in these days of Holy Week, into something beyond any calculable value. Therefore it is either nonsense or the only source of all real value. We cannot turn the Passion of Jesus into a platitude. It is too close for comfort. It makes or it breaks us. Perhaps, year by year, as we enter into this symbolic labyrinth, we only get so far before we draw back. But, year by year, we make a little advance on the previous year.

As with our meditation. It is a journey we make incrementally, integrating all we have learned before we can let it go and be led into the next phase. The world into which the experience of Jesus leads us is a world where the poor are enriched and the rich discover the freedom that poverty gives. Where poverty is the capacity for everything. And everything means total non-possessiveness. The pope giving haircuts, showers, sleeping bags, and tours of the Vatican to the homeless in St. Peter's is a newsworthy sacrament of this. But even then, only a sign.

By the "experience" of Jesus we mean two things. The experience that Jesus personally had. And our experience of his experience. In these days we learn, both disturbingly and wonderfully, what the word *Christian* means. But again, as Rumi said, "Several words yet remain unsaid, but it is unseasonably late; whatever was omitted in the night I will complete tomorrow."[8]

TUESDAY OF HOLY WEEK
John 13:21–33, 36–38

"After saying this Jesus was troubled in spirit, and declared, 'Very truly, I tell you, one of you will betray me.' The disciples looked at one another, uncertain of whom he was speaking. One of his disciples—the one whom Jesus loved—was reclining next to him; Simon Peter therefore motioned to him to ask Jesus of whom he was speaking. So while reclining next to Jesus, he asked him, 'Lord, who is it?' Jesus answered, 'It is the one to whom I give this piece of bread when I have dipped it in the dish.' So when he had dipped the piece of bread, he gave it to Judas son of Simon Iscariot. After he received the piece of bread, Satan entered into him. Jesus said to him, 'Do quickly what you are going to do.' Now no one at the table knew why he said this to him. Some thought that, because Judas had the common purse, Jesus was telling him, 'Buy what we need for the festival'; or, that he should give something to the poor. So, after receiving the piece of bread, he immediately went out. And it was night. When he had gone out, Jesus said, 'Now the Son of Man has been glorified, and God has been glorified in him. If God has been glorified in him, God will also glorify him in himself and will glorify him at once. Little children, I am with you only a little longer. You will look for me; and as I said to the Jews so now I say to you, "Where I am going, you cannot come." . . . Simon Peter said to him, 'Lord, where are you going?' Jesus answered, 'Where I am going, you cannot follow me now; but you will follow afterward.' Peter said to him, 'Lord, why can I not follow you now? I will lay down my life for you.' Jesus answered, 'Will you lay down your life for me? Very truly, I tell you, before the cock crows, you will have denied me three times.'"

IT WAS NIGHT

Today we are asked to focus on what happened at the Last Supper. It is chiaroscuro—the stark confronting of darkness and light. Heavy shadows are shed.

Shadows happen when light meets a resistant object that refuses to be—or cannot be—transparent. This resistance is the ego, and poor Judas has become the universal symbol of it. With a heavy heart Jesus sees and tells his companions that he will be betrayed. He knows that his end must involve total rejection and abandonment. They don't say, "Never." They ask, "Who?" Each hopes it will not be himself.

Only young John, the "one whom Jesus loved" and who stood at the foot of the cross, could dare ask him, "Who?" Jesus gives a piece of bread to Judas—is it before or after his words of consecration (which don't occur in John's account)? Then Satan enters Judas. And "it is night" for this merry band of disciples; this wonderful community of ideals is about to explode. *Satan* means refusal, rejection, the solid resistance to the power of light that refracts it into dark shadow. In later Christian history it is called the Anti-Christ because it looks like acceptance and reverence but it is in fact as much the opposite of that as you can get.

Those whom Satan, in this sense, enters into don't even know it. That is why it is so terrifying and creepy and dangerous. The corruption of the best is the worst, and the worst will always find a way of justifying or celebrating itself. Betrayal is ugly and will always apply cosmetics. But dive into this shadow and you will find a strange glow. Rumi may have seen this when he said, "If you are Love's lover and in quest of Love, take a sharp dagger and cut the throat of bashfulness."[9]

In the challenging moment, however, the only way of protecting ourselves from this massive self-delusion is to be intimate with the truth, to rest our head on its breast. To allow ourselves to be the one whom the Truth loves. This resting, this allowing ourselves to be loved, this intimacy with the teacher that alone dissolves the ego, is the meaning of meditation in Christian faith.

WEDNESDAY OF HOLY WEEK
Matthew 26:14–25

"Then one of the twelve, who was called Judas Iscariot, went to the chief priests and said, 'What will you give me if I betray him to you?' They paid him thirty pieces of silver. And from that moment he began to look for an opportunity to betray him. On the first day of Unleavened Bread the disciples came to Jesus, saying, 'Where do you want us to make the preparations for you to eat the Passover?' He said, 'Go into the city to a certain man, and say to him, "The Teacher says, My time is near; I will keep the Passover at your house with my disciples."' So the disciples did as Jesus had directed them, and they prepared the Passover meal. When it was evening, he took his place with the twelve; and while they were eating, he said, 'Truly I tell you, one of you will betray me.' And they became greatly distressed and began to say to him one after another, 'Surely not I, Lord?' He answered, 'The one who has dipped his hand into the bowl with me will betray me. The Son of Man goes as it is written of him, but woe to that one by whom the Son of Man is betrayed! It would have been better for that one not to have been born.' Judas, who betrayed him, said, 'Surely not I, Rabbi?' He replied, 'You have said so.'"

I WILL KEEP THE PASSOVER AT YOUR HOUSE WITH MY DISCIPLES
Actually the scene today rubs our nose again in the shame of betrayal. It's clearly an important if nasty element of Holy Week's meaning that we are meant to face.

It's like raising a socially embarrassing topic in the conversation at a pleasant dinner. You risk becoming everyone's worst companion and never being invited out again. Like dropping a piece of food from your mouth on the floor, you kick it under the table rather than retrieving it and offering it to your neighbor.

So we'll avoid the topic of betrayal, which is a key to this story. Instead, let's remember the context, the meal and the companionship, however flawed and fragile. There are people who have a gift for creating these occasions. They manage the food and the table with just the right kind of symbolism—not too formal but not too casual. It's an increasingly rare gift, this art of hospitality that allows celebration and friendship to happen and be shared for the duration of the meal. Every such occasion is a kind of Eucharist.

Perhaps one reason why today the Eucharist has lost its meaning for people, and why religious ceremony seems so incomprehensible and such an empty game, is because we see food as an individual indulgence and not as a communal sharing. For many families, in the lands of affluence especially, to sit and eat and talk and to remain together until the end of the meal seems a quaint custom. There's always something else to do in my room—download something, watch something, communicate in some other media—and the community of the table seems far less interesting once you have eaten your fill.

Yet eating with others is what prayer is all about. It is the time—like meditating with others or celebrating a ritual as we will begin to do tomorrow—when we are fed and nourished by the one who is the food itself. We need to stay and wait and allow ourselves to be waited on. After all, it was the betrayer who was the first to leave the table. (Sorry for bringing this up again.)

HOLY THURSDAY
John 13:1–15

"Now before the festival of the Passover, Jesus knew that his hour had come to depart from this world and go to the Father. Having loved his own who were in the world, he loved them to the end. The devil had already put it into the heart of Judas son of Simon Iscariot to betray him. And during supper Jesus, knowing that the Father had given all things into his hands, and that he had come from God and was going to God, got up from the table, took off his outer robe, and tied a towel around himself. Then he poured water into a basin and began to wash the disciples' feet and to wipe them with the towel that was tied around him. He came to Simon Peter, who said to him, 'Lord, are you going to wash my feet?' Jesus answered, 'You do not know now what I am doing, but later you will understand.' Peter said to him, 'You will never wash my feet.' Jesus answered, 'Unless I wash you, you have no share with me.' Simon Peter said to him, 'Lord, not my feet only but also my hands and my head!' Jesus said to him, 'One who has bathed does not need to wash, except for the feet, but is entirely clean. And you are clean, though not all of you.' For he knew who was to betray him; for this reason he said, 'Not all of you are clean.' After he had washed their feet, had put on his robe, and had returned to the table, he said to them, 'Do you know what I have done to you? You call me Teacher and Lord—and you are right, for that is what I am. So if I, your Lord and Teacher, have washed your feet, you also ought to wash one another's feet. For I have set you an example, that you also should do as I have done to you.'"

He poured water into a basin and began to wash the disciples' feet

Jean Vanier calls this washing of the feet the lost sacrament. It seems very symbolic and that is how it has come to be performed by the pope or the parish priest with a selected group on the high altar. On Bere Island, where we hold our annual Easter retreat, we do it a little differently, as Jean taught us years ago. All the people in the island church, including the islanders and those on the retreat, are invited to form into small circles and, one after the other, to wash one another's feet. When each has had his or her feet washed and dried, he or she prays over the person who performed this gentle and intimate act.

A lot of people in the church, like Peter, resolutely do not want their feet washed. It probably seems embarrassing to them and an unnecessary way of prolonging the service. I am never very successful at persuading them otherwise, though each year I live in hope.

There are those who wash, those who are washed and there are those who neither wash nor are washed and merely watch. We are a culture of watchers. We have got used to watching nature programs on television and marveling at the wonders of the world from the security of our armchair. We can press pause at any time to go and make a cup of tea. We come back and press play and the world performs for us again. We are like an ancient emperor being entertained. Viewers and consumers but not explorers, not people who get their feet wet walking across boggy ground.

Today, we begin the three days that culminate in the event in whose light we are bathed but which we cannot understand. And which we will never even see unless we become participants.

These days can only be entered as a way of transformation through the door of faith. I don't mean you have to believe in all that is said about them. In our time, belief comes later. Faith is about openness, reverence, being there and staying. Then, at a certain moment, transcendence dawns and it all comes together. Belief then becomes relevant.

But we cannot truly be there and stay merely as observers, consumers, as part of an audience. We will not be able to touch reality unless we allow it to touch us, to wash over us. Participation—and meditation—is what turns darkness into light and opens the portals of grace.

As our Sufi friend Rumi says, "When the sun has arisen, where then remains night? When the army of grace has come, where then remains affliction?"[10]

GOOD FRIDAY
John 18:37—19:42

"Pilate asked him, 'So you are a king?' Jesus answered, 'You say that I am a king. For this I was born, and for this I came into the world, to testify to the truth. Everyone who belongs to the truth listens to my voice.' Pilate asked him, 'What is truth?' After he had said this, he went out to the Jews again and told them, 'I find no case against him. But you have a custom that I release someone for you at the Passover. Do you want me to release for you the King of the Jews?' They shouted in reply, 'Not this man, but Barabbas!' Now Barabbas was a bandit. Then Pilate took Jesus and had him flogged. And the soldiers wove a crown of thorns and put it on his head, and they dressed him in a purple robe. They kept coming up to him, saying, 'Hail, King of the Jews!' and striking him on the face. Pilate went out again and said to them, 'Look, I am bringing him out to you to let you know that I find no case against him.' So Jesus came out, wearing the crown of thorns and the purple robe. Pilate said to them, 'Here is the man!' When the chief priests and the police saw him, they shouted, 'Crucify him! Crucify him!' Pilate said to them, 'Take him yourselves and crucify him; I find no case against him.' The Jews answered him, 'We have a law, and according to that law he ought to die because he has claimed to be the Son of God.' Now when Pilate heard this, he was more afraid than ever. He entered his headquarters again and asked Jesus, 'Where are you from?' But Jesus gave him no answer. Pilate therefore said to him, 'Do you refuse to speak to me? Do you not know that

I have power to release you, and power to crucify you?' Jesus answered him, 'You would have no power over me unless it had been given you from above; therefore the one who handed me over to you is guilty of a greater sin.' From then on Pilate tried to release him, but the Jews cried out, 'If you release this man, you are no friend of the emperor. Everyone who claims to be a king sets himself against the emperor.' When Pilate heard these words, he brought Jesus outside and sat on the judge's bench at a place called The Stone Pavement, or in Hebrew Gabbatha. Now it was the day of Preparation for the Passover; and it was about noon. He said to the Jews, 'Here is your King!' They cried out, 'Away with him! Away with him! Crucify him!' Pilate asked them, 'Shall I crucify your King?' The chief priests answered, 'We have no king but the emperor.' Then he handed him over to them to be crucified. So they took Jesus; and carrying the cross by himself, he went out to what is called The Place of the Skull, which in Hebrew is called Golgotha. There they crucified him, and with him two others, one on either side, with Jesus between them. Pilate also had an inscription written and put on the cross. It read, 'Jesus of Nazareth, the King of the Jews.' Many of the Jews read this inscription, because the place where Jesus was crucified was near the city; and it was written in Hebrew, in Latin, and in Greek. Then the chief priests of the Jews said to Pilate, 'Do not write, "The King of the Jews," but, "This man said, I am King of the Jews."' Pilate answered, 'What I have written I have written.' When the soldiers had crucified Jesus, they took his clothes and divided them into four parts, one for each soldier. They also took his tunic; now the tunic was seamless, woven in one piece from the top. So they said to one another, 'Let us not tear it, but cast lots for it to see who will get it.' This was to fulfil what the scripture says, 'They divided my clothes among themselves, and for my clothing they cast lots.' And that is what the soldiers did. Meanwhile, standing near the cross of Jesus were his mother, and his mother's sister, Mary the wife of Clopas, and Mary Magdalene. When Jesus saw his mother and the disciple whom he loved standing beside her, he said to his mother, 'Woman, here is your son.' Then he said to the disciple, 'Here is your mother.' And from that hour the disciple took her into his own home. After this, when Jesus knew that all was now finished, he said (in order to fulfil the scripture), 'I am thirsty.' A jar full of sour wine was standing there. So they put a sponge full of the wine on a branch of hyssop and held it to his mouth. When Jesus had received the wine, he said, 'It is finished.' Then he bowed his head and gave up his spirit. Since it was the day of Preparation, the Jews did not want the bodies left on the cross during the sabbath, especially because that sabbath was a day of great solemnity. So they asked Pilate to have the legs of the crucified men broken and the bodies removed. Then the soldiers came and broke the legs of the first and of the other who had been crucified with him. But when they came to Jesus and saw that he was already dead, they did not break his legs. Instead, one of the soldiers pierced his side with a spear, and at once blood and water came out. (He who saw this has testified so that you also may believe. His testimony is true, and he knows that he tells the truth.) These things occurred so that the scripture might be fulfilled, 'None of his bones shall be broken.' And again another passage of scripture says, 'They will look on the one whom they have pierced.' After these things, Joseph of Arimathea, who was a disciple of Jesus, though a secret one because of his fear of the Jews, asked Pilate to let him take away the body of Jesus. Pilate gave him permission; so he came and removed his body. Nicodemus, who had at first come to Jesus by night, also came, bringing a mixture of myrrh and aloes, weighing about a hundred pounds. They took the body of Jesus and wrapped it with the spices in linen cloths, according to the burial custom of the Jews. Now there was a garden in the place where he was crucified, and in the garden there was a new tomb in which no one had ever been laid. And so, because it was the Jewish day of Preparation, and the tomb was nearby, they laid Jesus there."

A JAR FULL OF SOUR WINE WAS STANDING THERE.
SO THEY PUT A SPONGE FULL OF THE WINE ON A BRANCH OF
HYSSOP AND HELD IT TO HIS MOUTH.
WHEN JESUS HAD RECEIVED THE WINE, HE SAID,
"IT IS FINISHED."
THEN HE BOWED HIS HEAD AND GAVE UP HIS SPIRIT

Today we pass with Jesus from the garden where he is betrayed by Judas to the legal show during which he is denied by Peter, rejected by his compatriots, ridiculed by the occupying power, tortured and crucified.

His last words in this account are not a self-defense, not a speech, not an accusation but a bare statement that whatever purpose his life contained is now finished. They are ambiguous. Looking backward we might say, it's all over, an irredeemable failure. Looking forward we can understand it to mean that it's now complete, everything has been fulfilled as it was meant to be.

But the moment of death is a present moment, looking neither backward nor forward to pass judgment or to revive hope. An absolute stillness. This is why the details of this moment have such sharp definition, though it is not easy to say what they mean. The sponge, the wine, the hyssop. The profound yet ineffectual gesture of comfort to a dying man.

This is the Zenlike quality of the Passion of Jesus. It is vivid, as vivid and non-conceptual as our own suffering and desolation. Yet there is no false consolation, no "it will be all right" or shy half-embrace from an outsider. We are either inside or outside at this moment. And if we are on the inside, with him, in him in meditation, as he said he would remain in and with us, then this is not the moment for explanations. In church today we read the Gospel, we say the prayers. But the real reason we are there is to join the line of people who silently, voluntarily come out of their polite pews, walk down the aisle and kiss the cross on which he died.

HOLY SATURDAY
Mark 16:1–7

"When the sabbath was over, Mary Magdalene, and Mary the mother of James, and Salome bought spices, so that they might go and anoint him. And very early on the first day of the week, when the sun had risen, they went to the tomb. They had been saying to one another, 'Who will roll away the stone for us from the entrance to the tomb?' When they looked up, they saw that the stone, which was very large, had already been rolled back. As they entered the tomb, they saw a young man, dressed in a white robe, sitting on the right side; and they were alarmed. But he said to them, 'Do not be alarmed; you are looking for Jesus of Nazareth, who was crucified. He has been raised; he is not here. Look, there is the place they laid him. But go, tell his disciples and Peter that he is going ahead of you to Galilee; there you will see him, just as he told you.'"

WHEN THEY LOOKED UP, THEY SAW THAT THE STONE, WHICH WAS VERY LARGE, HAD ALREADY BEEN ROLLED BACK

No church today. We're in the departure lounge waiting for the plane to arrive that will take us away on the trip we've been looking forward to for as long as we can remember.

At the vigil tonight, we recall all the eons of our human waiting from the Big Bang, through our primitive societies and addiction to warfare, our gradual enlightenment, frequent relapses into barbarity and ultimately our meeting with our silent, loving, invisible source of being, at our own level and in the flesh. Time collapses in on itself without losing any of its meaning or vividness. For a moment we glimpse the coherence, the unity and the blessedness of all our experience. Even the worst is included and transformed. But it is a very large stone.

They say that, in the first version of Mark's Gospel, he left out the resurrection. Everybody knew that was what it was all about and that it was very difficult to put the resurrection into words. When the Gospels do speak about it, it is about how people experienced it, rather than what a camera would have captured had it been there. Intensely real details passed on by word of mouth over the decades before it was put into writing glow with a significance and a power beyond what they seem. The ordinary is transfigured by the real. The meaning and purpose of human existence reveals itself at a level deeper than thought and shows it to be the level at which the source of love, creative and redeeming love itself, is.

Part of us says—and that's all right—this is intriguing but, come off it, too good to be true. Grow up and be real. It's only a beautiful myth. Yet, if we deny its truth, we would be untrue to that part of us which is awakened and continues to be illuminated over the decades of our lives by this news. This is the part of us which reaches beyond ourselves and beyond the stars. It is the part of us that is touched by meditation.

He is Risen. Alleluia!

Today we get up early, even after the late vigil, and walk up to the ancient standing stone in the exact center of Bere Island. We wait for the sun to rise. Whether it is clear and we see the great golden globe float up over the horizon, reminding us that every sunrise is a miracle to behold and a wonder to enjoy; or whether it's cloudy and the light grows stronger but without the brilliance—either way it is the best of Easter services. We are one with the world and all its creatures, under the sun that shines on good and bad alike.

Today, it all comes together and makes sense—the asceticism of Lent, the daily meditation and our reading about the deep mysteries of the Eucharist, the cross and the empty tomb. Now we know that all these are experienced and practiced in the light of the one who shows us that death, the great enemy, the great fear, is only a short bridge, though a lonely one that we all have to cross. To feel the transmission of the good news of Easter is to grow free from that primal fear.

The resurrection is, like the healing miracles of Jesus, a reality that restores us to life as we should and can live it—without fear of death, without being controlled by shame, confident that we are welcome home and that we are prevented even from the self-rejection and self-destructiveness which is the darkest corner of our shadow side. As those on whom the light of the resurrection shines—simply because we turn toward it and allow it to—we live this life day by day in a new way.

Newness. The smell of fresh bread, the newborn lambs, the discovery of affinity with another—all new and yet, like the sun, always present. I will be with you until the end of time. I am going away. It is good for you that I am leaving you. But I will come back to you and then you will know...

Thank you for your companionship during these forty days and forty nights, for sharing these reflections and journeying to this Easter Day together. I hope you have started to meditate, and that it remains part of your life. The resurrection sends us back to live *this* life in a new way. Meditation is about accepting this invitation. Happy Easter, every day!

APPENDIX

Alternative Lenten readings
Sundays and Holy Saturday

The readings for Sundays and Holy Saturday in this book are those given by the Catholic Church for Year B, with occasional variations in length. The reading for Palm Sunday has been abridged. Here are the readings for Years A and C.

YEAR A
First Sunday of Lent
    Matthew 4:1–11
Second Sunday of Lent
    Matthew 17:1–9
Third Sunday of Lent
    John 4:5–42
Fourth Sunday of Lent
    John 9:1–41
Fifth Sunday of Lent
    John 11:1–45
Palm Sunday
    Matthew 21:1–11
Holy Saturday
    Matthew 28:1–10

YEAR C
First Sunday of Lent
    Luke 4:1–13
Second Sunday of Lent
    Luke 9:28–36

Third Sunday of Lent
  Luke 13:1–9
Fourth Sunday of Lent
  Luke 15:1–3, 11–32
Fifth Sunday of Lent
  John 8:1–11
Palm Sunday
  Luke 19:28–40
Holy Saturday
  Luke 24:1–12

Weekdays

The set readings for weekdays during Lent are the same for all years. This book follows those passages (with occasional variation in length), with the exception of the following prescribed reading not used in this book. The reading for Good Friday has been abridged.

Thursday, fourth week of Lent
  John 5:31–47

NOTES

1. For ways to experience the support of a community of meditators, visit the website www.wccm.org.
2. To understand this in terms of Jesus's teaching, look at the Sermon on the Mount in chapters 5—7 of Matthew's Gospel.
3. For a short introduction to meditation in the Christian tradition of prayer, see my book *Christian Meditation: Your daily practice* (London: Medio Media, 2001) or John Main's *The Gethsemane Talks* (London: Medio Media, 2007).
4. George Herbert (1593–1633), "The Flower."
5. William Blake (1757–1827), "Eternity."
6. Anonymous, *The Cloud of Unknowing* (London: HarperCollins, 2004).
7. Jalal al-Din Rumi, *Mystical Poems of Rumi*, edited by Ehsan Yarshater and Hasan Javadi and translated by A.J. Arberry (Chicago: University of Chicago Press, 2009), 88. Combined and Corrected edition with a new Foreword by Franklin D. Lewis ©2009 by the University of Chicago. Used by kind permission.
8. Rumi, *Mystical Poems of Rumi*, 58.
9. Rumi, *Mystical Poems of Rumi*, 58.
10. Rumi, *Mystical Poems of Rumi*, 59.